An Analysis of

Ikujiro Nonaka's

A Dynamic Theory of Organizational Knowledge Creation

Stoyan Stoyanov

Published by Macat International Ltd
24:13 Coda Centre, 189 Munster Road, London SW6 6AW.

Distributed exclusively by Routledge
2 Park Square, Milton Park, Abingdon, Oxon OX14 4RN
711 Third Avenue, New York, NY 10017, USA

Routledge is an imprint of the Taylor & Francis Group, an informa business

www.macat.com
info@macat.com

Cataloguing in Publication Data
A catalogue record for this book is available from the British Library.
Library of Congress Cataloguing-in-Publication Data is available upon request.
Cover illustration: David Newton

ISBN 978-1-912303-99-1 (hardback)
ISBN 978-1-912284-70-2 (paperback)
ISBN 978-1-912284-84-9 (e-book)

Notice
The information in this book is designed to orientate readers of the work under analysis,
to elucidate and contextualise its key ideas and themes, and to aid in the development
of critical thinking skills. It is not meant to be used, nor should it be used, as a
substitute for original thinking or in place of original writing or research. References and
notes are provided for informational purposes and their presence does not constitute
endorsement of the information or opinions therein. This book is presented solely for
educational purposes. It is sold on the understanding that the publisher is not engaged
to provide any scholarly advice. The publisher has made every effort to ensure that
this book is accurate and up-to-date, but makes no warranties or representations with
regard to the completeness or reliability of the information it contains. The information
and the opinions provided herein are not guaranteed or warranted to produce particular
results and may not be suitable for students of every ability. The publisher shall not be
liable for any loss, damage or disruption arising from any errors or omissions, or from
the use of this book, including, but not limited to, special, incidental, consequential or
other damages caused, or alleged to have been caused, directly or indirectly, by the
information contained within.

CONTENTS

THE MACAT LIBRARY

The Macat Library is a series of unique academic explorations of seminal works in the humanities and social sciences – books and papers that have had a significant and widely recognised impact on their disciplines. It has been created to serve as much more than just a summary of what lies between the covers of a great book. It illuminates and explores the influences on, ideas of, and impact of that book. Our goal is to offer a learning resource that encourages critical thinking and fosters a better, deeper understanding of important ideas.

Each publication is divided into three Sections: Influences, Ideas, and Impact. Each Section has four Modules. These explore every important facet of the work, and the responses to it.

This Section-Module structure makes a Macat Library book easy to use, but it has another important feature. Because each Macat book is written to the same format, it is possible (and encouraged!) to cross-reference multiple Macat books along the same lines of inquiry or research. This allows the reader to open up interesting interdisciplinary pathways.

To further aid your reading, lists of glossary terms and people mentioned are included at the end of this book (these are indicated by an asterisk [*] throughout) – as well as a list of works cited.

Macat has worked with the University of Cambridge to identify the elements of critical thinking and understand the ways in which six different skills combine to enable effective thinking.
Three allow us to fully understand a problem; three more give us the tools to solve it. Together, these six skills make up the **PACIER** model of critical thinking. They are:

ANALYSIS – understanding how an argument is built
EVALUATION – exploring the strengths and weaknesses of an argument
INTERPRETATION – understanding issues of meaning

CREATIVE THINKING – coming up with new ideas and fresh connections
PROBLEM-SOLVING – producing strong solutions
REASONING – creating strong arguments

To find out more, visit **WWW.MACAT.COM.**

CRITICAL THINKING AND "A DYNAMIC THEORY OF ORGANIZATIONAL KNOWLEDGE CREATION"

Primary critical thinking skill: REASONING
Secondary critical thinking skill: PROBLEM-SOLVING

Through his work "A Dynamic Theory of Organizational Knowledge Creation," Ikujiro Nonaka shows himself to be a logical scholar who uses strong arguments embedded in the Japanese culture (e.g., notions such as honor and duty) to show the role of tacit knowledge in organizational knowledge creation and management.

According to the author "The process of innovation is not simply information processing; it's a process to capture, create, leverage, and retain knowledge." This awareness empowered Nonaka to capitalize on his understanding of the tacitness of knowledge and theorize on the dynamic processes related to knowledge creation.

Nonaka assures readers that individuals are an integral part of the knowledge-creation process, but also asserts that organizations are active and dynamic parties that also have a leading role in the knowledge-creation process. He suggests that organizations and environments simultaneously influence knowledge creation, which the author highlights through the introduced knowledge-conversion framework. The strong theoretical reasoning illuminated in the work largely convinces readers and the extended scholarly community of the validity of Nonaka's stance.

As a critical thinker Nonaka's reasoning has strong implications for solving a problem that many organizations have been experiencing—namely declining rates of innovation. Nonaka is renowned for his ability to introduce the behavior and the practices of Japanese organizations to American scholars and managers. He uses his work to propose that identifying and nurturing the dialogue between explicit and tacit knowledge within organizations could guide managers' knowledge-creation strategies. Such strategies should, according to Nonaka, inevitably promote open communication and the smooth transfer of ideas.

ABOUT THE AUTHOR OF THE ORIGINAL WORK

Ikujiro Nonaka (1935) is a Japanese organizational theorist born in Tokyo. He is Professor Emeritus at the Graduate School of International Corporate Strategy of the Hitotsubashi University best. Nonaka is best known for his study of knowledge management, and the processes of knowledge creation and their impact on organizational learning and advancement.

ABOUT THE AUTHOR OF THE ANALYSIS

Stoyan Stoyanov was educated at the University of Edinburgh. His research focuses on overcoming difficulties in internationalization by theorizing on networks' facilitative functions that companies can capitalize on. Other research interests include the processes related to the reduction of liabilities of outsidership of individuals, newness, smallness and foreignness, and organizations, as well as how individuals embed themselves in new, local environments.

ABOUT MACAT

GREAT WORKS FOR CRITICAL THINKING

Macat is focused on making the ideas of the world's great thinkers accessible and comprehensible to everybody, everywhere, in ways that promote the development of enhanced critical thinking skills.

It works with leading academics from the world's top universities to produce new analyses that focus on the ideas and the impact of the most influential works ever written across a wide variety of academic disciplines. Each of the works that sit at the heart of its growing library is an enduring example of great thinking. But by setting them in context – and looking at the influences that shaped their authors, as well as the responses they provoked – Macat encourages readers to look at these classics and game-changers with fresh eyes. Readers learn to think, engage and challenge their ideas, rather than simply accepting them.

WAYS IN TO THE TEXT

KEY POINTS

* Ikujiro Nonaka is a Japanese organizational theorist, best known for his study of knowledge management.

* Nonaka's article outlines the creation of organizational knowledge through the ongoing conversion of tacit and explicit knowledge.

* The work suggests that identifying the dialogue between explicit and tacit knowledge could guide managers' knowledge-creation strategies.

Who is Ikujiro Nonaka?

Ikujiro Nonaka is a Japanese organizational theorist and Professor Emeritus at the Graduate School of International Corporate Strategy of the Hitotsubashi University. He is best known for his study of knowledge management.

Nonaka was born in 1935 in Tokyo and witnessed first-hand the defeat of his country during World War II.* The devastation the war wrought on Japan motivated Nonaka to explore how his country could adapt its technological and organizational skills. As a result, Nonaka was motivated to pursue and complete an undergraduate degree in political science at Waseda University in 1958. His early education allowed him to secure a job at the Fuji Electric company where he later initiated a management program that would promote the organizational skills he considered important for competitiveness. This experience and his natural curiosity motivated Nonaka to study the processes of knowledge creation and its impact on organizational learning and advancement.

Nonaka graduated with both an MBA and a PhD in Business Administration from the University of California, Berkeley. The thematic focus of his degrees suggests the author's practical orientation, which he brought back to Japan after graduation. Following a few academic posts, Nonaka became the research director of the Japanese National Institute of Science and Technology. There, he published his seminal work "A Dynamic Theory of Organizational Knowledge Creation" in 1994, which is believed to be not simply a by-product of the post-war environment in Japan, but also a crucial element contributing to its remedy. This is due to the strong positive influence that the introduced effective organizational learning mechanisms have on the social, the political, and the economic environments. The scholar's contribution within the field of organizational learning brought him international recognition, which is likely to last for generations to come.

What does "A Dynamic Theory of Organizational Knowledge Creation" say?

Nonaka's "A Dynamic Theory of Organizational Knowledge Creation" sought to answer an important question: "How do organizations process knowledge and, more importantly, how can they create new knowledge?"[1]

The peculiarities of the time when the text was written enhanced the significance of the question, as well as the potential value of its answer. Nonaka recognized that society had evolved into a "knowledge society." This concept denotes the constantly increasing importance of knowledge for the social and the business operations in the contemporary socio-economic environment. The social transformation necessitated a more in-depth understanding of the ways business organizations not only utilize available knowledge, but also generate novel knowledge. Knowledge generation within the company context is an important prerequisite for competitive advantage, as it is a crucial input for product and service innovation initiatives. In that sense, the core question that Nonaka asks regarding knowledge processing and creation is a timely one.

The emerged focal question is a natural outcome of prior discussions on knowledge processing and, in particular, how companies can operate with information more efficiently. Nevertheless, what makes Nonaka's work stand out is the shift of the focus away from *knowledge as an input* to organizations, into *knowledge as an output* from organizations.

The author adopts a very specific focus on a particular knowledge process (that of knowledge creation), which necessitated a specific approach to addressing the recognized research gap. To answer the question posed, Nonaka examined the interaction between organizations and the environments they operate in. "A Dynamic Theory of Organizational Knowledge Creation" suggests that both parties (organizations and environments) influence knowledge creation. For example, innovation is argued to be equally influenced by not only the knowledge inputs extracted from the environment, but also the way the collected knowledge is converted within the organization (i.e., socialized, externalized, combined, internalized, or the SECI* model).

"A Dynamic Theory of Organizational Knowledge Creation" introduced a dynamic model of organizational knowledge creation. This model encompasses core behavioral assumptions of how the flow of knowledge transfers between individuals, what the potential difficulties might be, and how this flow can be promoted within an organizational setting. The assumptions and the model introduced in the author's 1994 work possess significant implications for management practitioners. The model is generally intuitive and clearly exemplifies the different types of knowledge within organizational systems, namely explicit* and tacit.*

Understanding the types of knowledge, and the ways knowledge flows between individuals is central for initiating business capability and process improvement. This characteristic of Nonaka's work makes his theories highly practical and important for the improvement of not only social environments, but also business environments.

The title Nonaka selected suggests the practicality of the work; more specifically the presence of the word "dynamic" suggests different scenarios to be discussed in the text. The dynamism of theory allows managers to better relate their organization's position to one of the provided scenarios. The easy identification of the organizational position serves as the starting point for adopting and implementing the theoretical model (i.e., the SECI model) outlined in the text. Understanding the position is a prerequisite for accurately applying theory and identifying how to reach a better consolidation of knowledge—an aim that possesses implications for efficiency or innovation capability improvement in knowledge-intensive businesses.

Why does "A Dynamic Theory of Organizational Knowledge Creation" matter?

The focus of Nonaka's "A Dynamic Theory of Organizational Knowledge Creation" is on knowledge development and utilization in an organizational context. The work was introduced at a time when society had evolved into a "knowledge society."* This notion represents the continuously increasing importance of knowledge in the contemporary socio-economic environment. Peter Drucker recognized this social transformation as early as 1969,[2] which was then adopted in the research of authors such as Daniel Bell,[3] Alvin Toffler,[4] and others. However, knowledge continues to be of increasing importance even today. Thus, the research focus on organizational knowledge development and utilization continues to be valued in the contemporary research landscape.

The continued interest in organizational learning creates an intellectual setting that promotes the relevance of "A Dynamic Theory of Organizational Knowledge Creation." The author's work is considered a useful addition to the debate on how organizations operate with knowledge as it proves the foundations of a more in-depth understanding of the ways business organizations not only utilize available knowledge, but also generate novel knowledge.

Prior to Nonaka's contribution, most of the research in organizational learning has focused on how organizations process knowledge, while excluding the knowledge generation abilities that organizations may have. Raising and answering the important question, "how do organizations process knowledge and, more importantly, how do they create new knowledge," allowed the author to "stimulate the next wave of research on organizational learning."[5] Therefore, despite some criticism, Nonaka's positive influence on the development of the contemporary organizational learning* field remains undisputable. Further recognition of the author's status is *The Economist's* acknowledgement that he was a "management guru," in its list of the world's most influential management thinkers.

NOTES

1   I. Nonaka, "A Dynamic Theory of Organizational Knowledge Creation," *Organization Science* 5/1 (1994), 16.

2   P. F. Drucker, *The Age of Discontinuity; Guidelines to Our Changing Society* (New York: Harper & Row, 1969), 80.

3   D. Bell, *The Coming of Post-industrial Society; a Venture in Social Forecasting* (New York: Basic Books, 1973), 41.

4   A. Toffler, *Powershift: Knowledge, Wealth, and Violence at the Edge of the 21st Century* (New York: Bantam Books, 1990), 112.

5   See Arie Y. Lewin in the preface of "A Dynamic Theory of Organizational Knowledge Creation," for a statement supporting Nonaka's text; and I. Nonaka, "A Dynamic Theory of Organizational Knowledge Creation," *Organization Science* 5/1 (1994), 14.

SECTION 1
INFLUENCES

MODULE 1
THE AUTHOR AND THE
HISTORICAL CONTEXT

KEY POINTS

- Understanding the types of knowledge and how they flow between individuals is central for initiating business and process improvements.

- Nonaka viewed companies as parties that actively engage in the knowledge creation process.

- Nonaka's work is the product of the author's background and exposure to Japanese business practices.

Why Read This Text?

Ikujiro Nonaka's "A Dynamic Theory of Organizational Knowledge Creation" is seminal because it outlines an important area of discussion, namely the creation of organizational knowledge through the constant conversion of the two types of knowledge: tacit and explicit. The author believes that outlining the dialogue between explicit and tacit knowledge has the potential to guide managers' knowledge creation strategies.

The ongoing interest in organizational learning creates an intellectual context that highlights the relevance of "A Dynamic Theory of Organizational Knowledge Creation." It is considered a useful addition to the debate on how organizations operate with knowledge as it proves the foundations of a more in-depth understanding of the ways business organizations not only utilize available knowledge, but also produce new knowledge.

Nonaka's interpretation on knowledge creation is centered on the belief that companies are not passive parties that simply utilize existing

> 66 The ever increasing importance of knowledge in contemporary society calls for a shift in our thinking concerning innovation in large business organizations—be it technical innovation, product innovation, or strategic or organizational innovation. It raises questions about how organizations process knowledge and, more importantly, how they create new knowledge. 99
>
> Ikujiro Nonaka, "A Dynamic Theory of Organizational Knowledge Creation"

knowledge for providing solutions to the customers. Instead, he believes that organizations and environments simultaneously influence knowledge creation. This suggests that it is not only the original knowledge that is valuable, but also the subsequent one, shaped by the intra-organizational processes: socialization, externalization, combination and internalization,* which is often referred to by its acronym: SECI.

The text is considered fundamental for the knowledge management field and as such, it has been thoroughly examined by a large number of academics. A search with Google Scholar reveals more than 14,000 citations in past and recent academic developments.

Author's Life

Nonaka is a renowned Japanese organizational theorist, who extensively explored the field of knowledge management. The single most important event that influenced the life and the career aspirations of the scholar can be traced to Japan's defeat in World War II. Nonaka witnessed first-hand how the war destroyed his country. He felt a strong moral obligation to explore how the country could adapt its technological and organizational skills to improve its social and economic condition. This goal motivated him to advance in his studies and graduate first from Waseda University in 1958 with a degree in political science, and then with an MBA and PhD in Business Administration from the University of California, Berkeley.

In addition, Nonaka always sought ways to apply his thinking on actual companies and thus improve their organizational skills and capabilities. For example, he joined the Fuji Electric company and initiated a management program to promote the company's competitiveness, which he felt was the only way to achieve nation-wide competitiveness. The author's strong, practical approach caught the attention of the Japanese National Institute of Science and Technology, which named him the director of research.

Author's Background

Ikujiro Nonaka's "A Dynamic Theory of Organizational Knowledge Creation" was the product of the author's background and exposure to Japanese business practices. American scholars and managers at the time were interested in works that illustrated the behavior, as well as the practices, of Japanese organizations. This interest was a result of the established acceptance of Japanese organization's reputation as leaders of innovation.

The country-specific origin of "A Dynamic Theory of Organizational Knowledge Creation" raises the question of whether or not the work is applicable to other business environments, different from the Japanese one.[1] There are two explanations why the context that inspired Nonaka should not be taken as a limitation.

First, the author was exposed to both the Japanese and the US educational systems and business environments, which gave him the ability to cross-fertilize ideas from different cultures. Moreover, the field of knowledge creation within corporations was also novel for the management study field in Japan, as well as in the US. Thus, Nonaka's efforts were on the development of the field of knowledge creation, irrespective of geographical location.

Second, central to Nonaka's belief, as observed from his research during the 1990s, is that the utilization and the generation of knowledge is how organizations build competitive advantage* irrespective of their origin. Globalization forces bring all organizations to the same market where they compete for shared, often scarce resources, legitimacy, and customers. As a result, the objective of organizations from all parts of the world is to be competitive and successful. Thus, if a given core Japanese cultural characteristic makes one organization more successful (e.g., the tendency of individuals to highly commit to an organizational goal), hypothetically, similar supportive and developmental organizational contexts can be purposefully built by managers in the west.

NOTES

1   M. Glisby and N. Holden, "Contextual Constraints in Knowledge Management Theory: the Cultural Embeddedness of Nonaka's Knowledge Creating Company," *Knowledge and Process Management* 10/1 (2003): 29.; M. Easterby-Smith, "Organizational Learning and National Culture: Do Models of Organizational Learning Apply Outside the USA?," *Boletin de Estudios Economicos* 53/164 (1998), 281.

MODULE 2
ACADEMIC CONTEXT

KEY POINTS

- Nonaka found that the intellectual environment in the twentieth century did not have an adequate understanding of how innovations occur.
- Polanyi's 1958 book *Personal Knowledge* was instrumental for the development of Nonaka's work.
- Nonaka's work relates to the increasing importance, and even necessity, of knowledge in society at the time.

The Work in its Context

A key concept in Ikujiro Nonaka's "A Dynamic Theory of Organizational Knowledge Creation" is tacitness.* This concept, which refers to what is implied or inferred without direct expression, is embedded in the Japanese culture, where notions such as honor, duty, and other traits are difficult to transfer to others.[1]

Although well-placed in the academic context and the literature, there are claims in support of the originality of Nonaka's thinking. In an interview conducted by C. Otto Scharmer* on the issue of knowledge creation,[2] the author raises these claims himself. During the interview, Nonaka claims that after attending a workshop on productivity and innovations at the Harvard Business School, he found that the intellectual environment at that time did not have an adequate understanding of how innovations occur. According to the author, "The process of innovation is not simply information processing; it's a process to capture, create, leverage, and retain knowledge."[3] This awareness empowered Nonaka to capitalize on his understating of the

> 66 It is widely observed that the society we live in has been gradually turning into a 'knowledge society'.... The ever increasing importance of knowledge in contemporary society calls for a shift in our thinking concerning innovation in large business organizations. 99
>
> Ikujiro Nonaka, "A Dynamic Theory of Organizational Knowledge Creation"

tacitness of knowledge and theorize on the dynamic processes related to knowledge creation.[4]

Michael Polanyi's* 1958 book *Personal Knowledge: Towards a Post-Critical Philosophy* was also instrumental in the development of Nonaka's "A Dynamic Theory of Organizational Knowledge Creation."[5] Nonaka builds upon Polanyi's work and takes it in a more practical direction through the consideration of not only personal knowledge as a source of knowledge creation, but also knowledge exchange in an organizational/social context. This created a strong fit for the article in the intellectual environment of the time. What clearly exemplifies Nonaka's addition to the academia is summed up in this statement: "Knowledge is alive because it changes continuously... transferred through human interaction."[6] This stance sets the foundation of a new dominant ideology, which promotes the belief that knowledge creation is dynamic in nature. It is created during the interplay of the processes of socialization, externalization, combination, and internalization (SECI).

Overview of the Field

The roots of the organizational learning field can be traced back many years before Nonaka's seminal work emerged. Researchers have previously identified that the marketplace influences the strategy-making process of corporations, which use their experience to build new assumptions and better reflect the changes in the market environment.[7] This can be considered as a form of experience-based learning, yet, the scholars at the time did not ask the precise questions that a contemporary organizational learning scholar would. For example, it was not clear how people interpreted previous experiences, scanned the current situation, considered options, and implemented decisions—thus, we cannot conclude whether the learning is based on trial and error or on an intentional/strategic one. Peter Senge and his colleagues started to look for evidence of creative learning by considering how teams brainstorm scenarios and consider best and worst options based on the proposed actions.[8]

Examining mental models within teams was the first step to shedding light on the organizational learning phenomenon. Nevertheless, the element of culture was largely missing in this theorization. Organizational learning needs to show evidence of how organizational culture predetermines decision inputs or perhaps the decisions made within the organization stem from power dynamics or past precedents.

The literature on this theme developed quickly after the publication of Senge's 1990 work on the "Art and Practice of the Learning Organization." As suggested by Philip Mirvis* "over 100 articles and several books have followed, not to mention newsletters, conferences, on-line news groups, and a practitioner's field book."[9]

Academic Influences

The core idea in "A Dynamic Theory of Organizational Knowledge Creation" is the creation of organizational knowledge through the constant conversion of the two types of knowledge, which the author outlines as tacit and explicit. The theme discussed in this work fits well in the intellectual preoccupations of the period. Starting from Peter Drucker,[10] Daniel Bell,[11] and later Alvin Toffler,[12] the issues of the period relate to the increasing importance, and even necessity, of knowledge in society. Nonaka relates to this issue by defining the society we live in as a "knowledge society." The importance of knowledge in the everyday business and social operations (e.g., in product and organizational innovations) defines Nonaka's ambition to disentangle the processes of knowledge creation.

The author is particularly interested in the organizational context of knowledge creation and knowledge processing. The author views the organizational context as a suitable domain for clearly illustrating the interrelatedness of tacit and explicit knowledge. Because of the clarity of the resulting knowledge creation framework, managers find it easily applicable to multiple organizational contexts. Thus, not surprisingly, business professionals involved in knowledge-intensive industries emerged as the major audience for Nonaka's research. In addition, managers in knowledge-intensive organizations are the author's intended audience, as Nonaka's academic and professional background holds a firm practical orientation.

NOTES

1   I. Nonaka and N. Konno, "The Concept of 'Ba': Building a Foundation for Knowledge Creation," *California Management Review* 40/3 (1998), 41.

2   C. O. Scharmer, "Conversation with Ikujiro Nonaka," *Reflections: The SoL Journal* 2/2 (2000), 24.

3   I. Nonaka and D. J. Teece, *Managing Industrial Knowledge: Creation Transfer and Utilization* (London: SAGE, 2001), 73.

4   Von Krogh, "Care in knowledge creation," *California Management Review* 40 (1998): 140.

5   M. Polanyi, *Personal Knowledge; Towards A Post-Critical Philosophy* (Chicago: University of Chicago Press, 1958), 124.

6   I. Nonaka, "A Dynamic Theory of Organizational Knowledge Creation," *Organization Science* 5/1 (1994), 16.

7   A.S. Huff, (Ed.) *Mapping Strategic Thought* (Chichester: Wiley, 1990).

8   P Senge, C. Roberts, R. Ross, B. Smith and A. Kleiner. *The Fifth Discipline Fieldbook* (New York, NY: Doubleday, 1994).

9   Philip H. Mirvis, "Historical Foundations of Organization Learning," *Journal of Organizational Change Management* 9/1 (1996), 15.

10 P. F. Drucker, The Age of Discontinuity; Guidelines to Our Changing Society (New York: Harper & Row, 1969), 81.

11 D. Bell, *The Coming of Post-industrial Society; a Venture in Social Forecasting* (New York: Basic Books, 1973), 36.

12 A. Toffler, *Powershift: Knowledge, Wealth, and Violence at the Edge of the 21st Century* (New York: Bantam Books, 1990), 112.

MODULE 3
THE PROBLEM

KEY POINTS

- Nonaka asks the question how can organizations process and operationalize knowledge into innovative business activities.
- Nonaka's work contributes to sociology, economics, and management science—disciplines interested in knowledge transfer and creation.
- Nonaka successfully extracts knowledge from the field of cognitive psychology and applies it to the discussion on organizational learning.

Core Question

Ikujiro Nonaka's "A Dynamic Theory of Organizational Knowledge Creation" emerged in a time characterized by the evolution of the society into a "knowledge society."* This term represents the constantly increasing significance of knowledge for the social and the business operations in the contemporary socio-economic environment. That transformation naturally influenced the intellectual debates of the time. The emerging questions utilized by scholars were within the locus of how organizations can process and implement knowledge into innovative business activities.

Nonaka's work focuses on the study of knowledge processing and knowledge creation within organizations. This key area of investigation emerged naturally from the prevalent scholarly discussions at the time. In the beginning, the general debate was motivated by the objective to understand the prerequisites for efficient information management during turbulent times. Nonaka acknowledged the importance of the

> **"** It raises questions about how organizations process knowledge and, more importantly, how they create new knowledge. Such a shift in general orientation will involve, among other things, a reconceptualization of the organizational knowledge creation processes. **"**
>
> Ikujiro Nonaka, "A Dynamic Theory of Organizational Knowledge Creation"

debate but recognized a problem that hindered the value of the discussion. The problem was that organizations lacked the research they needed to be active and dynamic parties in the knowledge creation process.

Nonaka's interpretation of knowledge creation was centered around the belief that companies are not passive parties that simply utilize existing knowledge for providing solutions to the market. Rather, he believed organizations and environments simultaneously influence knowledge creation. This suggests that it is not only the original knowledge that is valuable, but also the subsequent one, shaped by the intra-organizational processes: socialization, externalization, combination, and internalization (SECI).

The Participants
The origin of the processes for organizational knowledge creation that Nonaka isolated in "A Dynamic Theory of Organizational Knowledge Creation" can be traced to some fundamental research accounts developed by cognitive scientists. For example, in his book, *The Acquisition of Strategic Knowledge*, Thomas R. Gruber emphasized the importance of experts' "strategic knowledge."[1] Experts' strategic knowledge guides the actions undertaken by the actors (such as developing tools for knowledge acquisition). The process of developing tools for knowledge acquisition can be regarded as knowledge creation per se. This suggests that knowledge processing

seldom occurs without the creation of new knowledge. Therefore, knowledge conversion within organizations is an important component for the dynamic knowledge creation process.

Another scholar who Nonaka shows similar research orientation to is Michael Polanyi, who introduced the concept of tacit knowledge in his 1958 book *Personal Knowledge*.[2] Although Nonaka cites Polanyi's work, he takes it in a more practical direction through the consideration of not only personal knowledge as a source of knowledge creation, but also knowledge exchange in an organizational/social context.

This broader theme of tacit knowledge, which emerged from the work of cognitive scientists (e.g., Polanyi), when combined with Nonaka's dynamic understanding of the organization, resulted in the actual knowledge conversion mechanisms (i.e., SECI) that take place in an organizational context. As a result, Nonaka's work has implications for a wide range of disciplines such as sociology, economics, and management science, whose objectives involve understanding knowledge transfer and creation.

The Contemporary Debate

Basing his research orientation on the prior work of Drucker,[3] Bell,[4] and Toffler[5] on "knowledge society,*" Nonaka naturally called for more attention to be focused on understanding the ways business organizations not only utilize available knowledge, but also generate such via knowledge conversion mechanisms. The author clearly states that the origin of the idea for conversion of knowledge comes from the field of cognitive psychology, beginning with the work of John Robert Anderson[6] who introduced the Adaptive Control or Thought or ACT* model, a model used to divide knowledge into declarative knowledge* (i.e., actual knowledge) and procedural knowledge* (i.e., methodological knowledge, like riding a bike).

In a similar way, Nonaka adopts Polanyi's division of knowledge into explicit* and tacit* knowledge,[7] attributable to declarative and procedural knowledge respectively. The tangent point between Anderson* and Nonaka's research gets more noticeable when introducing Anderson's hypothesis that the transformation between the two types of knowledge is not only possible, but also necessary for the development of cognitive skills.* The development of cognitive skills is equivalent to knowledge development on an individual level, while Nonaka's contribution focuses on the development of cognitive skills within the organization, i.e., organizational capabilities.

Although "A Dynamic Theory of Organizational Knowledge Creation" shares core ideas and is conceptually similar to Anderson's, Nonaka brings an important addition to prior knowledge. The contribution that the SECI framework makes to ACT is the hypothesis that the knowledge conversion is not unidirectional.* Thus, the conversion does not occur only from explicit to tacit knowledge, but also from tacit to tacit (socialization), from tacit to explicit (externalization), from explicit to explicit (combination), and from explicit to tacit knowledge (internalization).

Nonaka's work successfully extracts knowledge from the field of cognitive psychology and applies it to the discussion on organizational learning. This provoked a positive response from the scholarly community. For example, Arie Y. Lewin* states in the foreword of "A Dynamic Theory of Organizational Knowledge Creation" that Nonaka's contribution "has the potential to stimulate the next wave of research on organizational learning."[8] This response is a strong recognition of the merits of the theory emerging at this time.

NOTES

1   T. R. Gruber, *The Acquisition of Strategic Knowledge* (Boston: Academic Press, 1989), 12.

2   M. Polanyi, *Personal Knowledge: Towards A Post-Critical Philosophy* (Chicago: University of Chicago Press, 1958), 124.

3   P. F. Drucker, *The Age of Discontinuity: Guidelines to Our Changing Society* (New York: Harper & Row, 1969), 66.

4   D. Bell, *The Coming of Post-industrial Society: A Venture in Social Forecasting* (New York: Basic Books, 1973), 41.

5   A. Toffler, *Powershift: Knowledge, Wealth, and Violence at the Edge of the 21st Century* (New York: Bantam Books, 1990), 112.

6   J. R. Anderson, *The Architecture of Cognition* (Cambridge: Harvard University Press, 1983), 27.

7   M. Polanyi, *Personal Knowledge*, 124.

8   A.Y. Lewin in "A Dynamic Theory of Organizational Knowledge Creation," *Organization Science* 5/1 (1994), 1.

MODULE 4
THE AUTHOR'S CONTRIBUTION

KEY POINTS

- Nonaka introduces the idea that knowledge in organizations is shaped by the ongoing dialogue between explicit and tacit knowledge.

- The introduced framework illustrates the ways tacit and explicit knowledge are converted through the use of four methods.

- It can be argued that Nonaka's theory often remains inaccessible for managers, yet highly appreciated by academics.

Author's Aims

Ikujiro Nonaka's "A Dynamic Theory of Organizational Knowledge Creation" serves as a conduit of his main goal: to facilitate the management of the organizational knowledge creation process. Nonaka intended to introduce the idea that knowledge in organizations is shaped by the ongoing dialogue between explicit and tacit knowledge. The author believed that outlining the interchange and the possible relationship between the two types of knowledge has the potential to guide managers' knowledge-creation strategies.

The author's aim to facilitate knowledge creation resulted in the development of a coherent theoretical framework founded upon the conversion of tacit and explicit knowledge (i.e., tacit to tacit knowledge transfer, tacit to explicit knowledge transfer, explicit to tacit knowledge transfer, and explicit to explicit knowledge transfer). The plan behind the introduction of the theoretical framework was to provide a clear

> ❝ It is argued that while new knowledge is developed by individuals, organizations play a critical role in articulating and amplifying that knowledge. A theoretical framework is developed which provides an analytical perspective on the constituent dimensions of knowledge creation. ❞
>
> Ikujiro Nonaka, "A Dynamic Theory of Organizational Knowledge Creation"

analytical perspective with enhanced explanatory power that can be perceived equally well by researchers as well as practitioners.

The importance of having both academics and practitioners adopt his ideas relating to managing organizational knowledge stems from Nonaka's belief that knowledge creation can be promoted within an organizational setting. Thus, practitioners can focus their efforts on designing institutional environments and crafting policies that promote innovation and knowledge creation.

Approach

Nonaka largely addresses his aim by providing a framework that illustrates the ways tacit and explicit knowledge can be converted through the use of four conversion methods (socialization, externalization, combination, internalization). The SECI process is an original piece of work in that it explains knowledge generation as a product of the interaction between explicit and tacit knowledge.

Nonaka expresses the above superordinate ideas of the text in a very systematic way. Simultaneously, the author highlights the interrelatedness of the components and the processes relevant to their conversion. This enriches readers' understanding of the knowledge creation as a holistic practice as opposed to a sum of distinct processes.

Without doubt, the author's background adds to his academic credibility and shapes his approach to discussing organizational learning. Coming from Japan, Nonaka's national and cultural affiliations have visible influences on his academic reputation. His exposure to the Japanese business and cultural environment, as well as the North American one, allowed him to bridge the initial gap between the two environments—something that was rare at the time. For that reason, the incorporation of the Japanese practices for innovation in the North American research context was looked upon favorably by scholars.

It is exactly the incorporation of the Japanese practices for innovation that constitute the specific approach of the author and the originality of his work "A Dynamic Theory of Organizational Knowledge Creation." Nonaka's interpretation of knowledge-creation processes reflects the methods he had observed in Japan. The originality is centered around the belief that companies are not passive parties that simply utilize existing knowledge for providing solutions to the customers. What set Nonaka's ideas apart from the organizational theorists of the time was the belief that organizations and environments simultaneously shape knowledge creation. Thus, it is not only the original knowledge that is valuable, but also the subsequent one, shaped by the intraorganizational processes: socialization, externalization, combination, and internalization.

Contribution in Context

Although the explanatory power of Nonaka's "A Dynamic Theory of Organizational Knowledge Creation" is strengthened by the well-structured knowledge conversion framework, the theory often remains inaccessible for managers. This impedes full understanding and implementation of Nonaka's work in an organizational context. In fact, Nonaka acknowledged this problem in the preface of a follow-up work, "Enabling Knowledge Creation," where he wrote, "it was not as helpful as it might have been in telling readers how to go about actually creating knowledge."[1] This remark suggests that more work needs to be done before practitioners interested in increasing their organizations' knowledge creation prospects can execute this theoretical framework.

The root of the problem can be traced back to the author's heavy use of abstract concepts, which managers might find difficult to understand. Another factor that may further increase the theory's ambiguity is the lack of openly testable hypotheses, the addition of which would have increased preciseness and, possibly, the theory's execution.

Despite these issues, Nonaka was still successful in realizing his primary objective of introducing the importance of the dialogue between explicit and tacit knowledge for knowledge creation. Indeed, Arie Y. Lewin made this point in the foreword of "A Dynamic Theory of Organizational Knowledge Creation," writing: "I recommended this paper to *Organization Science* readers because I believe that it has the potential to stimulate the next wave of research on organization learning."[2]

NOTES

1   G. Krogh, and K. Ichijo, *Enabling Knowledge Creation: How to Unlock the Mystery of Tacit Knowledge and Release the Power of Innovation* (Oxford: Oxford University Press, 2000), 35.

2   A.Y. Lewin in "A Dynamic Theory of Organizational Knowledge Creation," *Organization Science* 5/1 (1994), 1.

SECTION 2
IDEAS

MODULE 5
MAIN IDEAS

KEY POINTS

- Nonaka studies knowledge conversion using the modes of knowledge socialization, externalization, combination, and internalization.

- Knowledge creation depends on the ability of organizations to promote open communication and transfer of ideas.

- The intended audience of the work is not only members of the academic scholarship, but also management professionals.

Key Themes

The core themes of Ikujiro Nonaka's "A Dynamic Theory of Organizational Knowledge Creation" are knowledge creation and the active role of organizations in this process. The author scrutinizes knowledge conversion during the modes of knowledge socialization, externalization, combination, and internalization (SECI) that take place in the organizational context.

Although a central part of the text, the discussion on knowledge conversion is preceded by a number of other themes. As the author states, "basic concepts and models of the theory of organizational knowledge creation are presented."[1] This logical arrangement has the purpose of familiarizing readers with the origin and the conceptual foundations of the major contribution (i.e., the SECI model). The flow of themes follows the order from general to specific, which allows the central contribution to emerge as a justified true belief.

The author starts with clarifying the difference between knowledge and information. Nonaka utilizes relevant literature to

> **❝** It can be argued that the organization's interaction with its environment, together with the means by which it creates and distributes information and knowledge, are more important when it comes to building an active and dynamic understanding of the organization. For example, innovation, which is a key form of organizational knowledge creation, cannot be explained sufficiently in terms of information processing or problem solving. **❞**
>
> Ikujiro Nonaka, "A Dynamic Theory of Organizational Knowledge Creation"

relate information to the "flow of messages."[2] In a broad sense, information is defined as a bundle of data with a particular relevance. On the other hand, knowledge is defined as a justified true belief. The author relates knowledge to human action, which suggests the role of individuals in the knowledge-creation process.

What follows is a classification of knowledge into two distinct categories: explicit and tacit. The first represents the type of knowledge that can be easily codified and transferred from one person to another. The second type has distinct characteristics that make it difficult for transferring between people. However, due to the difficulty of communicating tacit knowledge, it is often recognized as the foremost reason for an organization's competitive advantage.

Referring back to the relationship between knowledge and human action, and the role of individuals in the knowledge creation, Nonaka introduces the discussion of another important theme, namely individuals' commitment. The core of the theme is the question of how to encourage individuals' commitment to knowledge creation within the organizational context. The presented factors that induce individuals' commitment are intention,* autonomy,* and fluctuation.*

All of the themes above fit well together and provide solid conceptual and theoretical foundations that precede the introduction of the modes of knowledge creation (i.e., socialization, externalization, combination, and internalization). The gradual introduction of Nonaka's theoretical contribution to the knowledge-creation literature convinces readers that his framework represents new *knowledge** (i.e., justified true belief), as opposed to *information.**

Exploring the Ideas

Nonaka's main idea is centered on the belief that companies are not passive parties that simply utilize existing knowledge, but they can actively engage in knowledge generation. The author highlighted that organizations and environments simultaneously influence knowledge creation through the conversion of tacit and explicit knowledge from one form to another, explained below:

Socialization is defined as the transfer between an individual's tacit knowledge to another's. Individuals' knowledge is gradually transferred to the group and eventually melts into the organizational knowledge. That relocation takes place in the course of the social blend of the members via habitual interaction and through sharing the same organizational beliefs and routines. Not only does the internal socialization help in the transfer of tacit knowledge, but also through participation in joint activities or simply sharing the same.

Externalization entails the conversion of tacit knowledge into explicit knowledge, as this is an easier to understand form of knowledge that facilitates the transfer of personal and professional knowledge to others. This is also asserted by Joseph Raelin,*[3] who gives the example of a professor's knowledge that needs to be externalized for the students to have a full grasp on the presented material. Therefore, externalization eases the process of knowledge utilization while providing a larger community of individuals who enjoy enhanced ease of access to, and understanding of, knowledge.

Combination entails the enrichment of, and the resulting generation of, more profound, explicit knowledge. Combination builds upon a certain cluster of knowledge by integrating other relevant knowledge. It contributes to the knowledge within the organization and often transcends the group whose knowledge has been combined.

Internalization is defined by Nonaka as the conversion of explicit knowledge into tacit knowledge. In internalization, action and practice are the main holders of explicit knowledge. The individuals who obtain that knowledge will gain from the experience of the ones who went through the difficult process of acquiring it. Tacit knowledge, on the other hand, could be acquired through internalization processes such as personal meetings, on-the-job training, etc. (e.g., by reading or listening to others' stories or through simulating their actions).

Language and Expression

Nonaka introduced a number of themes in his work "A Dynamic Theory of Organizational Knowledge Creation." All of the introduced themes add to the overall argument that organizations have an active role in knowledge creation and process. Thus, the intended audience of the work is not only members of the academic scholarship, but also management professional.

The discussion of the themes: knowledge and information, explicit and tacit knowledge, as well as the role of individuals' commitment in the knowledge creation process, all laid the foundations for the most significant contribution that the author makes: the knowledge conversion framework. The framework is comprised of socialization, externalization, combination, and internalization, which take place in the organizational context.

The introduced themes fit well together because the author lays the arguments from general to specific, constantly building up on previous discussions. This arrangement allows the formation of a chain of evidence that is easily traceable and effortlessly followed by the reader. Thus, although the language of the work can be hard to understand due to the number of concepts, moving from general to specific, and clearly defining concepts facilitates the overall readability of the work.

Readers can easily adopt the interpretation that knowledge creation depends on the ability of the environment to promote open communication and transfer of ideas. However, readers with a professional management background may highlight the lack of specificity when it comes to the application of the framework to corporate policymaking. Managers may find themselves struggling to develop organizational strategies that would promote the open communication and smooth transfer of ideas that Nonaka actively endorses.

NOTES

1   I. Nonaka, "A Dynamic Theory of Organizational Knowledge Creation," *Organization Science* 5/1 (1994): 10.

2   Nonaka, "A Dynamic Theory of Organizational Knowledge Creation," 11.

3   J. Raelin, "Work-based learning in practice," *Journal of Workplace Learning* 10 (1997), 280.

MODULE 6
SECONDARY IDEAS

KEY POINTS

- An important subordinate idea stemming from Nonaka's work is how to trigger changes in the organization's wider knowledge systems.

- Nonaka suggested that companies can benefit from promoting *creative chaos, redundancy of information,* and *requisite variety.*

- The origin of knowledge remains underexplored and scholars often adopt the simplistic view that knowledge stems from the individual.

Other Ideas

Along with the main idea of the creation of organizational knowledge via the constant conversion of knowledge, "A Dynamic Theory of Organizational Knowledge Creation" also showcases Ikujiro Nonaka's secondary ideas, which deserve thorough examination as they add to the work's potential to "stimulate the next wave of research on organization learning."[1]

One of these important ancillary ideas is how to "trigger changes in the organization's wider knowledge systems."[2] Building on this idea is closely related to the realization of innovations in organizations through abandoning or altering already established and well-rooted production or service delivery practices via "unlearning." The idea of triggering organizational change precedes the knowledge-conversion practices that can occur in organizations. The first focuses on "enabling conditions that promote a more favorable climate for effective knowledge creation."[3] The second focuses on the knowledge-creation

66 The redundancy of information refers to the existence of information more than the specific information required immediately by each individual. The sharing of extra information between individuals promotes the sharing of individual tacit knowledge. Since members share overlapping information, they can sense what others are trying to articulate. 99

Ikujiro Nonaka, "A Dynamic Theory of Organizational Knowledge Creation"

processes. These ideas combine to produce something greater than the sum of their parts, namely a holistic understanding of both the conditions and the processes for knowledge generation to take place within organizations.

Although less central, the idea of triggering change by improving the organizational climate is considered another "practical perspective on the management of organizational knowledge creation."[4] The origin of "unlearning,"* also known as "double-loop learning,"* are traceable to the work of Argyris and Schon,[5] and Hedberg,[6] respectively. Nonaka enriches the discussion by providing particular conditions that improve the knowledge-generating climate in organizations. The stated conditions are *creative chaos*, *redundancy of information,* and *requisite variety*. The author believes that realizing these within the organizational context will increase the individuals' commitment to knowledge generation.

Exploring the Ideas

Nonaka has suggested that realizing *creative chaos*, *redundancy of information,* and *requisite variety* within the organizational context will increase the individuals' commitment to knowledge generation. Below, you can see these ideas explored further.

Creative chaos occurs naturally in moments of rapid and unpredictable change, often when companies do not know how to react to sudden loss of competitive advantage. Nonaka claims that this condition can actually promote knowledge generation if managers realize that the "old order" (i.e., the organizational infrastructure) needs to be updated. This idea stems from the concept "order out of noise" introduced by Von Foerster.[7] The notion behind it is that simulating organizational crises may promote the generation of new solutions to not-yet-existing problems. This may lead to new efficiencies and competitive advantage.

Redundancy of information refers to the ability to obtain given information from multiple sources within the organization. The availability of multiple repositories of information or knowledge is believed to improve the control over knowledge creation. Moreover, organizational infrastructure that allows for redundancy of information may lead to "various combinations of information flexibility,"[8] thus promoting innovations. Redundancy of information can be achieved by stimulating internal competition or establishing job rotation* within organizations.

Redundancy of information is an important condition for knowledge generation but it may also inhibit the interaction between employees as the information processing time is reduced. Redundancy impedes the possibility to come up with new interpretations of existing knowledge. To control for that, Nonaka introduces Ashby's concept "requisite variety,"[9] which suggests that maximizing organizational efficiency is possible when individuals "are not loaded with information in the excess of each one's cognitive capacity."[10] The practical realization of this concept involves having employees who are known by others for their expertise in a given domain.

By introducing the above ideas, Nonaka has provided his academic successors with a scheme for further research. However, the usefulness of the author's contribution goes beyond academics. It reaches practitioners by outlining the possible steps for the execution of *creative chaos*, *redundancy of information,* and *requisite variety*.

Overlooked

"A Dynamic Theory of Organizational Knowledge Creation" raises an important question: how do organizations process knowledge and, more importantly, how do they create new knowledge? Posing this question, and actively contributing towards the answer, places Nonaka's work at the center of the organizational learning field. Due to its important role, this work has been thoroughly examined by a large number of academics.[11] However, there is an important aspect of the work that did not draw much scholarly attention: the origin of knowledge.

Scholars appear to have neglected this theme, having often adopted the interpretation that all knowledge stems from the individual.[12] Nonaka agrees that individuals play an important role by stating, "the prime mover in the process of organizational knowledge creation is the individual,"[13] but he does not undermine the important role of groups in the knowledge creation process and proposes that "although ideas are formed in the minds of individuals, interaction between individuals typically plays a critical role in developing these ideas."[14] Despite this, "much of the literature on management and organization theory has treated tacit knowledge on the 'individual' level."[15]

For that reason, it seems evident that the central theme that remained partially neglected is looking at knowledge creation as a process dependent on the iteration of communities.

The reason why the scholarly community missed the importance of the idea that "communities of interaction" can be the conflicting messages that the author sent by abovementioned statements. Nonaka's followers paid limited attention to this suggestion and continued to focus predominantly on the core output of the article, namely the understanding that business organizations not only utilize available knowledge, but also generate such via knowledge conversion mechanisms.

To overcome any potential theoretical bias, Nonaka attempted to refocus audience's attention on the role of groups in the knowledge creation process. He did so by introducing the concept of "quality of group tacit knowledge" in an article published in 2008.[16] Although Nonaka tried to refocus the attention of the community to this aspect of his initial work, the article is currently cited only 116 times since its publication. For that reason, the idea that knowledge stems from groups remains secondary and rather neglected.

NOTES

1 A statement made by Arie Y. Lewin in the preface of Nonaka's work "A Dynamic Theory of Organisational Knowledge Creation."; I. Nonaka, "A Dynamic Theory of Organizational Knowledge Creation," *Organization Science* 5/1 (1994), 16.

2 Nonaka, "A Dynamic Theory of Organizational Knowledge Creation," 15.

3 Nonaka, "A Dynamic Theory of Organizational Knowledge Creation," 27.

4 Nonaka, "A Dynamic Theory of Organizational Knowledge Creation," 15.

5 C. Argyris and D.A. Schön. *Organizational Learning*. (Reading: Addison-Wesley Pub. Co., 1978).

6 B. L. T. Hedberg, "How Organizations Learn and Unlearn," in *Handbook of organizational design*, ed. P. C. Nystrom and W. H. Starbuck (Oxford: Oxford University Press, 1981), 77.

7 H. Von Foerster, "Principles of Self-organization in a Socio-Managerial Context," in *Self-organization and Management of Social Systems*, ed. H. Ulrich and G. J.B. Probst (Berlin: Springer-Verlag, 1984), 93.

8 Nonaka, "A Dynamic Theory of Organizational Knowledge Creation," 29.

9 W. R. Ashby, *An introduction to Cybernetics* (London: Champan & Hall, 1956), 100.

10 Nonaka, "A Dynamic Theory of Organizational Knowledge Creation," 29.

11 More than 14,000 citations upon a Google Scholar search.

12 Z. Erden, G. Krogh and I. Nonaka, "The Quality of Group Tacit Knowledge," *Journal of Strategic Information Systems* 17 (2008): 4.

13 Nonaka, "A Dynamic Theory of Organizational Knowledge Creation," 16.

14 Nonaka, "A Dynamic Theory of Organizational Knowledge Creation," 16.

15 Erden, Krogh and Nonaka, "The Quality of Group Tacit Knowledge," 4.; S. Gourlay. "Towards Conceptual Clarity for 'Tacit Knowledge': A Review of Empirical Studies," *Knowledge Management Research & Practice*, 4 (2006):60–69.

16 Erden, Krogh and Nonaka, "The Quality of Group Tacit Knowledge," 4.

MODULE 7
ACHIEVEMENT

KEY POINTS

- Nonaka's work has gained a paradigmatic status in the knowledge management discipline.
- Knowledge conversion is found to be highly applicable in the context of the teaching training programs.
- The extensive explanatory power of Nonaka's contribution in field beyond management adds to the perceived merits of the work.

Assessing the Argument

Overall, the core ideas presented in Ikujiro Nonaka's "A Dynamic Theory of Organizational Knowledge Creation" are a natural result of the author's exposure to numerous national, cultural, educational, and business affiliations. For that reason, the ideas put forth in his work are not original to his bibliography, but rather form a consistent flow of research outputs within the field of organizational knowledge creation. Perhaps this is why, since its publication in 1994, "A Dynamic Theory of Organizational Knowledge Creation" has gained a paradigmatic status in the knowledge management discipline.[1] Nonaka's central contribution is the SECI model, which introduces the theoretical assumption that knowledge creation is shaped through constant social interactions both inside and outside of organizations. This idea has been regularly incorporated in studies that go beyond the immediate field of knowledge management.[2] Other fields where the text's contributions have been utilized reside in broader learning contexts, such as organizational learning, organizational development, and education.

> ❝ It should be stressed that the principles described have a more general application to any organization, either economic or social, private or public, manufacturing or service, in the coming age despite their field of activities as well as geographical and cultural location. ❞
>
> Ikujiro Nonaka, *A Dynamic Theory of Organizational Knowledge Creation*

As Maltiadis Lytras* and his colleagues have suggested, the fact that knowledge is so important in every strand of society suggests that a company's understanding of the knowledge generation process can be transferable in others contexts.[3] In addition, Kairit Tammets* suggests that Nonaka's contribution are applicable to a wide range of disciplines because the "understanding of the interplay between the management of knowledge and learning is strategically important for creating and maintaining effective learning processes in a large variety of non-traditional learning situations."[4]

Achievement in Context

Estimating the achievement and originality of Nonaka's thinking within the context of broader academic works is a challenging endeavor, largely because of the widespread recognition of the importance of this text.

According to Nonaka, "[the] process of innovation is not simply information processing; it's a process to capture, create, leverage, and retain knowledge."[5] All of these processes that Nonaka could identify in the social and business networks in Japan, but not in the US.[6]

Nonaka is one of the first organizational management scholars to apply Japanese organizational knowledge and culture to the US context. The incorporation of Japanese practices for innovation enhancement involved overcoming the restrictions related to shifting academic knowledge from outside the US, as well as having it accepted by management scholars. Nonaka overcame this restriction by doing something unusual for a Japanese researcher at that time, namely publishing in Western journals, such as *Organization Science*, where "A Dynamic Theory of Organizational Knowledge Creation" first appeared.[7]

Something that highlights Nonaka's achievement in the broader scholarly context is that studies interested in the processes of learning have not adapted his SECI model. Instead, the model has been directly applied to illustrate that individuals in every context within the knowledge society "need to adapt themselves to the changing environmental conditions and thus increase organizational responsiveness."[8]

One such context in which knowledge conversion is found to be highly applicable is in teaching training programs. The application of the SECI knowledge management model to teaching training is believed to facilitate teachers' ability to "identify, create, represent, distribute, and enable the adoption of good teaching practices in collaborative settings."[9]

The fact that the model's explanatory power has been applied in contexts that stray from the organizational sphere has legitimized the conversion of tacit and explicit knowledge as an integral part for the exploration of learning.[10] The extensive explanatory power of Nonaka's contribution adds to the perceived merits of his article.

Limitations

In "A Dynamic Theory of Organizational Knowledge Creation," Nonaka offers a reconceptualization of the processes related to knowledge creation. The author suggests a dynamic approach to knowledge creation via the constant conversion of explicit and tacit knowledge in an organizational setting, as opposed to the previous rather static approach. Nonaka's research perspective is inspired by

Japan's business culture in which strong social ties are conduits for knowledge exchange and conversion.[11] Tacit knowledge plays an important role in Nonaka's knowledge conversion framework, nevertheless this type of knowledge is very difficult to transfer from one person to another. Despite this, it is known that tacit knowledge is most easily transferred via established social networks.[12] The existence of such strong interpersonal networks is a fundamental part of Japanese culture. Therefore, by bringing conclusions from the Japanese business context, Nonaka has offered the rest of the world the chance to learn more about the source of Japan's competitive advantage in innovations.

The newly introduced knowledge creation perspective has been well accepted by the Western intellectual community because of its powerful practice implications. The high practicality of the Japanese model of knowledge creation is justified by the immense success in innovation that the Japanese automobile industry has had internationally. In that sense, the economic environment in the US created the need for such research that would allow the country to regain its position in the competitive knowledge–intensive industries.

NOTES

1   M. Easterby-Smith and M. Lyles, "Introduction: Watersheds of Organizational Learning and Knowledge Management," in *The Blackwell Handbook of Organizational Learning and Knowledge Management*, ed. M. Easterby-Smith and M. Lyles (Oxford: Blackwell Publishing, 2003), 7.

2   K. Tammets, "Meta-Analysis of Nonaka & Takeuchi's Knowledge Management Model in the Context of Lifelong Learning," *Journal of Knowledge Management Practice* 13/4 (2012): 1.

3   M. D. Lytras, A. Naeve and A. Pouloudi. "Knowledge Management as a Reference Theory for E-learning: A Conceptual and Technological Perspective," *International Journal of Distance Education Technologies*, 3/2 (2005): 1–12.

4   Tammets, "Meta-Analysis of Nonaka & Takeuchi's Knowledge Management," 1.

5   I. Nonaka and D. J. Teece, *Managing Industrial Knowledge: Creation Transfer and Utilisation* (London: SAGE, 2001), 73.

6   I. Nonaka, "A Dynamic Theory of Organizational Knowledge Creation," *Organization Science* 5/1 (1994), 16.

7   "AIB Fellow - Ikujiro Nonaka," Academy of International Business (AIB), accessed September 2, 2017, http://aib.msu.edu/Fellow/192/Ikujiro-Nonaka.

8   Tammets, "Meta-Analysis of Nonaka & Takeuchi's Knowledge Management," 1.

9   Y. C. Yeh, L. Y. Huang and Y. L. Yeh. "Knowledge Management in Blended Learning: Effects on Professional Development in Creativity Instruction," *Computers & Education*, 56 (2011), 146–156.

10 Tammets, "Meta-Analysis of Nonaka & Takeuchi's Knowledge Management," 1.

11 Nonaka, "A Dynamic Theory of Organizational Knowledge Creation," 16.

12 D. Skyrme, "Developing a knowledge strategy: From management to leadership," in *Knowledge Management: Classic and Contemporary Works*, eds. D. Morey, M. Maybury, and B. Thuraisigham (Cambridge: MIT Press, 2000), 61.

MODULE 8
PLACE IN THE AUTHOR'S WORK

KEY POINTS

- Nonaka's work is a product of a mature thinker, who started his publishing track in 1974.

- There is a need for elaborating on the dynamics that comprise effective knowledge management and how to embed them in business organizations.

- The text is an output of the unification of Western and Eastern scholarship in an attempt to create a global intellectual domain.

Positioning

Ikujiro Nonaka's "A Dynamic Theory of Organizational Knowledge Creation" was published in 1994 in the journal *Organization Science*. The text is a product of a mature thinker, who has, since 1974, published many academic works in both Japan and the US. Despite the duality of his research pipeline, Nonaka's investigations have always been guided by his interest in organizational knowledge management. For that reason, when "A Dynamic Theory of Organizational Knowledge Creation" first appeared in 1994, it was a comprehensive and well-argued perspective that successfully spurred the dialogue about the importance of dynamic approaches to knowledge creation.

The continuous upgrading of the author's ideas (achieved by adding factors that increase our understanding of dynamic knowledge creation and management), creates a solid research corpus.[1] The influence of Nonaka's corpus is further augmented by the constant incorporation of different views via co-authorship. In this way, the author not only benefits from adding more like-minded scholars who

> **❝** By concentrating on the concept of organizational
> knowledge creation, it has been possible to develop a
> perspective which goes beyond straightforward notions
> of 'organizational learning'. **❞**
>
> Ikujiro Nonaka, *A Dynamic Theory of Organizational Knowledge Creation*

will sustain his legacy, but also operationalizes his main belief, namely that knowledge is created through the continuous conversion of tacit and explicit knowledge that takes place in a dialogue between individuals.

Integration

Despite its apparent comprehensiveness and acceptance, "A Dynamic Theory of Organizational Knowledge Creation" is in need of further answers about the dynamics that comprise effective knowledge management and how to embed them in business organizations. Due to the growing interest, Nonaka used the SECI model proposed in "A Dynamic Theory of Organizational Knowledge Creation" as a foundation for his subsequent works. In this way, the author did not modify his prior conclusions, but rather enriched the acceptance of his theory that knowledge creation is a dynamic process. As a result, many factors had to be considered. Nonaka's subsequent research corpus focused on how organizations can build competitive advantage by better managing the dynamism of the knowledge-related processes, a question that continues to engage managers.

A good illustration of the cohesiveness of Nonaka's corpus is his article, "SECI, Ba and Leadership: A Model of Dynamic Knowledge Creation,"[2] where the author uses concepts emerging from his prior works to reveal how organizations *create, maintain,* and *exploit* knowledge in a dynamic manner. The elements that the author uses are the SECI process,[3] the Ba,* and the role of the managers (i.e., leadership).

Significance

Nonaka remained true to this way of creating knowledge. He applied this vision throughout his own career by working closely with many different scholars among whom were Hirotaka Takeuchi,* Ryoko Toyama,* Katsuhiro Umemoto,* Noboru Konno,* Ken Kusunoki,* and others. The dialogue of the importance of explicit and tacit knowledge conversion for innovation creation, which Nonaka spurred in the scholarly community, made him an established and well-accepted scholar.

Another reason for Nonaka's acceptance in the Western intellectual environment is the significance of the Japanese cultural, academic, and business environment, which was to a great extent still closed at the time. Despite being relatively inaccessible, Japanese intellectual environment was of great interest to the rest of the world since the global success of the Japanese automobile industry.

According to Nonaka's Academy of International Business profile, his "detailed studies of product development in Japanese companies" is what really attracted the interest of Western scholars.[4] This suggests the importance of Japan in a research context. In addition, according to the profile, it was unusual for a Japanese researcher at that time to publish in Western research publications like *Organization Science*, where "A Dynamic Theory of Organizational Knowledge Creation" first appeared.

Thus, the work and its significance appear to be a product of the exposure of a Japanese scholar to the Western intellectual environment. It represents the unification of Western and the Eastern scholarship for the creation of a global intellectual domain.

NOTES

1   I. Nonaka, R. Toyama, and N. Konno, "SECI, Ba and Leadership: A Unified Model of Dynamic Knowledge Creation," *Long Range Planning* 33/1 (2000), 5.

2   Nonaka, Toyama, and Konno, "SECI, Ba and Leadership", 5.

3   I. Nonaka, "A Dynamic Theory of Organizational Knowledge Creation," *Organization Science* 5/1 (1994), 16.

4   Academy of International Business (AIB), "AIB Fellow - Ikujiro Nonaka," accessed September 2, 2017, http://aib.msu.edu/Fellow/192/Ikujiro-Nonaka.

SECTION 3
IMPACT

MODULE 9
THE FIRST RESPONSES

KEY POINTS

- Nonaka's argumentation is logical, yet, critics can request a more nuanced consideration of knowledge and its conversion processes.

- Nonaka was asked to show empirically how we can distinguish among the four classes of knowledge conversion.

- It cannot be claimed that any consensus between critics and Nonaka has been achieved.

Criticism

Ikujiro Nonaka's "A Dynamic Theory of Organizational Knowledge Creation" introduces key arguments that add to the organizational learning* literature. The most notable contribution of Nonaka's work is the SECI framework for knowledge conversion, which is continuously being cited by representatives of an increasing number of disciplines. Nevertheless, the SECI framework has never been supported by empirical evidence, which has allowed critics to challenge its coherence.

Even though the key argument of Nonaka's work is logical, it is possible for critics to request a more nuanced consideration of knowledge and the related conversion processes. This appears to attract the most criticism. For example, Paul Adler* criticized Nonaka's static consideration of the nature of explicit and tacit knowledge.[1] The SECI framework is argued to be dynamic, thus Adler expects a more visible contrast between the types of knowledge and a detailed discussion on the potential inter-relatedness. In addition,

> ❝ As knowledge emerges as an ever more important feature of advanced industrial development, it is necessary to pay increased attention to the processes by which it is created and the assessment of its quality and value both to the organization and society. ❞
>
> Ikujiro Nonaka, "A Dynamic Theory of Organizational Knowledge Creation"

Adler argued that the SECI modes of knowledge creation discussed in "A Dynamic Theory of Organizational Knowledge Creation" have been explored in the context of other fields. These developments have been overlooked in the text, which may result in a limited understanding of the considered modes.

Another strand of criticism stems from René Jorna,* whose argument is based on the study of semiology.*[2] René Jorna viewed SECI modes as vague and suggested the development of an additional framework that clarifies how we can distinguish among the four classes of knowledge conversion. Although not present in literature, such classification is believed to strengthen the theoretical robustness of the SECI model.

Responses

Although Nonaka's text is considered an important contribution to the development of organizational learning literature,[3] it does not escape criticism. Challenges from scholars like Adler and Jorna motivated Nonaka to revisit the knowledge creation theory. The most visible effort to address some of the criticism is the work, "The Knowledge-Creating Theory Revisited: Knowledge Creation as a Synthesizing Process," published in 2003, in cooperation with Ryoko Toyama.*[4]

The authors' response includes a number of clarifications, which were meant to rebut some of the criticism; however, it remains possible that Nonaka and Toyama did not provide direct answers to criticism but rather attempted to reaffirm the credibility of the SECI framework.

For example, Adler's criticism of Nonaka's static consideration of the nature of explicit and tacit knowledge receives little attention. Based on this limitation, Adler argued whether the SECI framework is indeed dynamic. Nonaka and Toyama's reply excluded the demand for a more visible differentiation between tacit and explicit knowledge and a discussion on their potential inter-relatedness. Yet, they defend the dynamism of the SECI model by providing a narrower explanation of the nature of its dynamism, arguing that the model is dynamic in contrast with existing theories. Moreover, the SECI model employs a consideration of the interaction between the organization and the environment over time.[5] This consideration allows light to be shed on the interaction of organizational knowledge creation and its utilization.

Another strand of criticism emerged from Jorna, who viewed the SECI modes as vague.[6] Jorna demanded that Nonaka show empirically how to distinguish among the four classes of knowledge conversion through the use of the actual semantics of individuals involved in the organizational knowledge conversion. Jorna believed that such classification would strengthen the theoretical robustness of the SECI model. However, Nonaka appeared less receptive to this line of argument, and so Jorna's criticism did not result in any noticeable revisions.

Conflict and Consensus

Overall, Nonaka's work has attracted little systematic criticism since its publication. However, this does not mean that the above outlined criticism should not be taken seriously. In fact, these critiques motivated Nonaka to revisit the knowledge creation theory. The attempt to address the challenges appeared through the work "The Knowledge-creating Theory Revisited: Knowledge Creation as a Synthesizing Process," published in 2003 in cooperation with Ryoko

Toyama. The authors' first sentence makes a clear statement: "This paper is a part of our attempt to build a new knowledge-based theory of the firm and organization to explain the dynamic process of knowledge creation and utilization." Therefore, the criticism had a clear influence on the evolution of Nonaka's theoretical contribution.

It cannot be claimed, however, that any consensus between critics and the authors has been achieved. In Nonaka and Toyama's article they admit that "we are still far from understanding the process in which an organization creates and utilizes knowledge."[7] Nevertheless, they see that "management scholars and practitioners often fail to understand the essence of the knowledge-creating process"[8] as the reason for this lack of theoretical advancement. This statement suggests the confidence that the Nonaka has in the explanatory power of the SECI model and its importance for the organization learning field.

NOTES

1 P. S. Adler, "Comment on I. Nonaka: Managing innovation as an organizational knowledge creation process," in *Technology Management and Corporate Strategies: a Tricontinental Perspective*, ed. J. Allouche and G. Pogorel (Amsterdam: Elsevier, 1995), 110.

2 R. Jorna, "Managing Knowledge," *Semiotic Review of Books* 9/2 (1998): 5.

3 A statement supporting the ideas is made by Arie Y. Lewin in the preface of "A Dynamic Theory of Organizational Knowledge Creation."; I. Nonaka, "A Dynamic Theory of Organizational Knowledge Creation," *Organization Science* 5/1 (1994), 14.

4 I. Nonaka and R. Toyama, "The Knowledge-Creating Theory Revisited: Knowledge Creation as a Synthesizing Process," *Knowledge Management Research & Practice* 1 (2003), 2.

5 Nonaka and Toyama, "The Knowledge-Creating Theory Revisited," 3.

6 R. Jorna, "Managing Knowledge," *Semiotic Review of Books* 9/2 (1998), 5.

7 Nonaka and Toyama, "The Knowledge-Creating Theory Revisited," 2.

8 Nonaka and Toyama, "The Knowledge-Creating Theory Revisited," 3.

MODULE 10
THE EVOLVING DEBATE

KEY POINTS

- It is possible to trace the influence Nonaka's modes of knowledge creation imposed on subsequent studies within different disciplines.

- Nonaka is renowned for his ability to introduce the practices of Japanese organizations to American scholars and managers.

- It may not come as a surprise that many contemporary academic works are founded on the research ideas discussed by Ikujiro Nonaka.

Uses and Problems

It is possible to trace the influence that each one of the modes of knowledge creation proposed in "A Dynamic Theory of Organizational Knowledge Creation" imposed on subsequent studies within the broader organizational learning discipline. This approach means to illustrate both how well-integrated Nonaka's ideas continue to be, as well as the degree to which his work revolutionized the intellectual environment.

Nonaka is renowned for introducing the behavior and practices of Japanese organizations to American scholars and managers. Nevertheless, the strong demand to further understand the Japanese business models, origin of knowledge, and business strategies persisted even after the publication of the work "A Dynamic Theory of Organizational Knowledge Creation." The strong demand naturally created more supply and the people who captured this market were other Japanese authors such as M. Kodama, R. Toyama, N. Konno, and others.

> **"** The theory of organizational knowledge creation proposed here has been constructed mainly on the basis of hands-on research and practical experience of Japanese firms. Nevertheless, it should be stressed that the principles described have a more general application. **"**
>
> Ikujiro Nonaka, "A Dynamic Theory of Organizational Knowledge Creation"

These scholars were inspired by the important question that Nonaka raised, namely: how do organizations process knowledge and, more importantly, how do they create new knowledge?[1] Following Nonaka, the scholarly community's interpretation of knowledge creation began to center around the belief that organizations and environments simultaneously influence knowledge creation. For that reason, it is not surprising that the knowledge conversion processes (i.e., SECI) shaped subsequent research. Together, these scholars reshaped the organizational-learning school of thought and embedded a new research direction that diverges from the notion that organizations are passive knowledge recipients.

The research of Kodama, Toyama, and Konno contributed an important aspect to Nonaka's ideas in "A Dynamic Theory of Organizational Knowledge Creation."[2] They were motivated to examine the dynamism of the knowledge-creation process. Empirically strengthening the emphasis on the dynamism of the knowledge-creation process was an important mission taken by Kodama.[3] This addressed the pending remarks from Adler, who criticizes Nonaka's static consideration of the nature of explicit and tacit knowledge in the SECI framework.[4] Adler expected a more visible empirical contrast between the types of knowledge and a detailed discussion on the potential inter-relatedness, certainly a merit of Kodama's work.

Overall, Nonaka managed to outline an area of discussion (i.e., knowledge generation), which proved over time to be of high importance for the scholarly community. The author fueled a wide intellectual focus on knowledge generation within an organizational context, which was a change from the historic view that organizations simply utilize knowledge. As suggested by Arie Y. Lewin, "A Dynamic Theory of Organizational Knowledge Creation" is without any doubt a game changer because it "stimulated the next wave of research on organizational learning."[5]

Schools of Thought

Nonaka's main idea is centered on the belief that companies are not passive parties that simply utilize existing knowledge, but that they can actively engage in knowledge generation. The author highlights that organizations and environments simultaneously influence knowledge creation. This view on knowledge creation inspired a wave of scholars who adopted Nonaka's notion in order to build upon the organizational learning field.

Scholars adopted the perspective that knowledge creation depends on the ability of the organizations to promote open communication and idea transfer. Judy Gray* and Iain Densten[6] suggest that testing this assumption is possible by the integration of the SECI model with the Competing Values Framework* (CVF). Bringing this additional framework to the discussion is believed to clarify the influence of organizational culture on knowledge creation. The CVF advocates that informal interactions between individuals facilitate collective experiences to stimulate organizational effectiveness, in particular, knowledge communication and creation. Thus, "integrating the CVF with the SECI may enhance our understanding of the social processes that determine organizational effectiveness."[7] The application of critical apparatuses (e.g., CVF) allowed extending the author's ideas and gaining more nuanced and critical understanding of the merits of the work.

The formation of this school of thought led to the continuous enhancement of our knowledge on organizational learning. This development process also led to the recognition of the work's limitations and its inability to explain thoroughly the observed phenomenon (i.e., organizational learning).

The same limitation is highlighted by critics of "A Dynamic Theory of Organizational Knowledge Creation,"[8] who call Nonaka's model "simplistic" and unable to "codify everything" that may play a role in the organizational knowledge creation. Moreover, the critical understanding of the SECI model may be further driven by the consideration of its relevance in the current age of highly advanced information and communications technologies.[9]

To address this concern, as well as to add to the established school of thought, David Teece* takes the idea about the dynamism of knowledge conversion even further. He adds to the discussion on the dynamic capabilities* that organizations need to have in order to strategically execute knowledge conversion in a way that allows them to sense and then seize a market opportunity.

This is evidence that Nonaka's work "A Dynamic Theory of Organizational Knowledge Creation" serves as a solid conceptual and theoretical foundation for contemporary scholarly developments. Scholars have successfully grasped the author's legacy and have intertwined it with their own research ideas to stimulate the development of the organizational learning discipline.

In Current Scholarship

Many contemporary academic works are founded on and extend the research ideas discussed in Nonaka's "A Dynamic Theory of Organizational Knowledge Creation." Conducting a short literature review gives a clear idea of the proliferation of Nonaka's theoretical assumption that knowledge creation is shaped by the constant social interaction inside and outside of organizations. A distinctive mutual interest can be immediately identified in the work of Mitsuru Kodama, "Knowledge Creation through Networked Strategic Communities,"[10] which resides in the affirmation of Nonaka's ideas and extending their range.

Kodama adds a new context where the explanatory power of Nonaka's SECI model can be fully utilized—the context of networks. In this way, Kodama not only supports the centrality of the ideas in "A Dynamic Theory of Organizational Knowledge Creation," but also progressively introduces a more evolutionary understanding of the knowledge management discipline. Such cases of theoretical continuity prove the high academic relevance that Nonaka's work has for contemporary knowledge-related disciplines.

The belief that knowledge conversion within the network context leads to various forms of innovation is already well grounded.[11] Companies of all sizes need to continuously evolve through innovation if they want to maintain a sustainable competitive advantage. This requires constant knowledge conversion with an increasing number of parties in order to gain fresh insights and new ideas that can drive innovation. Conversion of knowledge with the same people over and over again will naturally reduce organizations' capabilities to innovate. Thus, although Nonaka's notion of knowledge conversion is faithfully embraced, its strategic relevance expands when contextualized in a constantly expanding network.

Getting embedded in networks allows transcending one's limited perspective and reaching out to new explicit or tacit knowledge. Establishing access to such knowledge serves as the prerequisite for dynamic knowledge creation. The fundamental role of Nonaka in the new intellectual movement (i.e., the role of networks in innovation) is highlighted by Nonaka's statement that tacit knowledge is most easily distributed in social networks.[12] Overall, the ease of the distribution of knowledge within networks and the need for exposure to new sources of information gave rise to the current research focus on networks as a path to knowledge creation.

NOTES

1   I. Nonaka, "A Dynamic Theory of Organizational Knowledge Creation," *Organization Science* 5/1 (1994), 16.

2   M. Kodama, "Knowledge Creation through Networked Strategic Communities: Case Studies on New Product Development in Japanese Companies," *Long Range Planning* 38 (2005): 27.; I. Nonaka and N. Konno, "The Concept of 'Ba': Building a Foundation for Knowledge Creation," *California Management Review* 40/3 (1998): 41.; I. Nonaka, R. Toyama and N. Konno. "SECI, 'Ba' and Leadership: A Unified Model of Dynamic Knowledge Creation," *Long Range Planning*, 33 (2000), 5-34.

3   Kodama, "Knowledge Creation Through Networked Strategic Communities," 27.

4   P. S. Adler, "Comment on I. Nonaka: Managing innovation as an organizational knowledge creation process," in *Technology Management and Corporate Strategies: a Tricontinental Perspective*, ed. J. Allouche and G. Pogorel (Amsterdam: Elsevier, 1995), 110.

5   Nonaka, "A Dynamic Theory of Organizational Knowledge Creation," 17.

6   J. H. Gray and I. L. Densten, "Towards an Integrative Model of Organizational Culture and Knowledge Management," *International Journal of Organizational Behaviour* 9/2 (2005), 594.

7   Gray and Densten, "Towards an Integrative Model of Organizational Culture and Knowledge Management," 594.

8   B. Sarayreh, A. Mardawi and R. Dmour, "Comparative Study: The Nonaka Model of Knowledge Management," *International Journal of Engineering and Advanced Technology* 1/6 (2012), 2249.

9   J. Essers and J. Schreinemakers, "Nonaka's Subjectivist Conception of Knowledge in Corporate Knowledge Program," *Knowledge Organization* 24/1 (1997): 24. C. Bereiter, *Education and Mind in the Knowledge Age.* (Mahwah, N.J.: L. Erlbaum Associates, 2002), 83.

10 M. Kodama, "Knowledge Creation through Networked Strategic Communities: Case Studies on New Product Development in Japanese Companies," *Long Range Planning* 38 (2005), 27.

11 Kodama, "Knowledge Creation through Networked Strategic Communities," 27.

12 Nonaka, "A Dynamic Theory of Organizational Knowledge Creation," 16.

MODULE 11
IMPACT AND INFLUENCE TODAY

KEY POINTS

- The transformation into "knowledge society" requires an understanding of how business organizations utilize and generate new knowledge.
- There is a lack of systematic confrontations between Nonaka's work and contemporary studies.
- Nonaka's work "A Dynamic Theory of Organizational Knowledge Creation" is no longer part of rigorous intellectual debates.

Position

Ikujiro Nonaka's "A Dynamic Theory of Organizational Knowledge Creation" was developed towards the end of the twentieth century. The article fully embraces the notion of a "knowledge society," a concept referring to the constantly increasing importance of knowledge in the socio-economic environment. Given that the importance of knowledge persists in our contemporary society, it is clear that Nonaka's contribution has preserved its relevance even today.

The sustained social transformation into "knowledge society" necessitated an in-depth understanding of the ways business organizations not only utilize knowledge, but also generate new knowledge. Since the publication of Nonaka's work in 1994, scholars have adopted this research direction. The ideas introduced in "A Dynamic Theory of Organizational Knowledge Creation" (e.g., the modes of knowledge conversion or SECI) have become the foundation of the contemporary organization learning school of thought, resulting in the ever-increasing timeliness of Nonaka's contribution.

> **❝** The key for this synergetic expansion of knowledge is joint creation of knowledge by individuals and organizations. In this sense, the theory of organizational knowledge creation is at the same time a basic theory for building a truly 'humanistic' knowledge society beyond the limitations of mere 'economic rationality'. **❞**
>
> Ikujiro Nonaka, "A Dynamic Theory of Organizational Knowledge Creation"

Time has had a positive influence on the credibility of "A Dynamic Theory of Organizational Knowledge Creation," because the idea that organizations are active participants in the knowledge generation process is now the norm.[1] Thus, there are no identifiable contemporary confrontations on this perspective.

Interaction

"A Dynamic Theory of Organizational Knowledge Creation" has become well-established in the management scholarly community. There have been some historic expressions of opinions that the work needs to dig even deeper into the knowledge creation realm. However, as the field progressed, it has become difficult to identify any opponents who completely disregard the intellectual insight the work has proposed. Standing against Nonaka's insight is likely to pose a threat to the credibility of the challenger.

One reason for the lack of systematic confrontations between Nonaka's work and contemporary studies is the fact that "knowledge management has gained its own academic legitimacy and paradigmatic status in such a short period of time, owing much to Nonaka's continued advancement of the field."[2] Thus, it seems that Nonaka has an important role in the foundation of the contemporary knowledge management field.

The on-going transformative power of the article can be traced to the constructive impact it had on contemporary management of knowledge work.[3] Followers remained true to the original spirit of the text (i.e., the notion that organizations are active participants in the knowledge-generation process).

The fit of Nonaka's work "A Dynamic Theory of Organizational Knowledge Creation" in the present intellectual environment seems indisputable. This is acknowledged by Michael Teece who claims that "there is no one who in recent years has done more to shape the field of [knowledge] management than Ikujiro Nonaka."[4]

The Continuing Debate

"A Dynamic Theory of Organizational Knowledge Creation" is no longer part of rigorous intellectual debates. The loss of centrality in debates, however, is not because of losing credibility, but because the article's merits in the field of knowledge management are so widely acknowledged. As a result, the notion that organizations are active participants in knowledge generation is now the norm.[5] Thus, there are no identifiable contemporary confrontations on this perspective.

The significant legitimacy of the author prevents major challenges to his work. There is a consensus that "knowledge management has gained its own academic legitimacy and paradigmatic status in such a short period of time, owing much to Nonaka's continued advancement of the field."[6] Thus, it is common that challenges are masked in the form of introducing a different viewpoint, extending, or revisiting his knowledge conversion model.[7]

The high status of the SECI knowledge conversion framework is another major demotivation that discourages potential challengers. Overall, the seminal article, "A Dynamic Theory of Organizational Knowledge Creation," has become more of a point of reference than a focus of battling schools of thought. For that reason, critics are careful when questioning such a well-established work and are careful to do it with the respect Nonaka's work is due. After all, the *Economist* even conferred on Nonaka the status of being a "management guru."[8]

NOTES

1   J. Hong, "Glocalizing Nonaka's Knowledge Creation Model: Issues and Challenges," *Management Learning* 0 (2011), 1.

2   Hong, "Glocalizing Nonaka's Knowledge Creation Model," 1.

3   M. Easterby-Smith and M. Lyles, "Introduction: Watersheds of Organizational Learning and Knowledge Management," in *The Blackwell Handbook of Organizational Learning and Knowledge Management*, ed. M. Easterby-Smith and M. Lyles (Oxford: Blackwell Publishing, 2003), 7.; D. Teece, "Foreword: From the Management of R and D to Knowledge," in *Managing Flow: A Process Theory of the Knowledge-based Firm*, ed. I. Nonaka, R. Toyama and T. Hirata (New York: Palgarve MacMillan, 2008), 3.

4   Teece, "Foreword: From the Management of R and D to Knowledge," 3.

5   J. Hong, "Glocalizing Nonaka's Knowledge Creation Model: Issues and Challenges," *Management Learning* 0 (2011), 1.

6   Hong, "Glocalizing Nonaka's Knowledge Creation Model," 1.

7   P. S. Adler, "Comment on I. Nonaka: Managing Innovation as an Organizational Knowledge Creation Process," in *Technology Management and Corporate Strategies: a Tricontinental Perspective*, ed. J. Allouche and G. Pogorel (Amsterdam: Elsevier, 1995), 110.; R. Jorna, "Managing Knowledge," *Semiotic Review of Books* 9/2 (1998), 5.

8   *The Economist* named Nonaka a "management guru" because of his significant contribution to the management science field.

MODULE 12
WHERE NEXT?

KEY POINTS

- Nonaka's knowledge conversion model is believed to be a valuable starting point for furthering learning and knowledge creation fields.

- The successful operation within a knowledge society needs to be an output of a collective action undertaken by different parties.

- Nonaka's work deserves special attention as it frames an important area of discussion, that of knowledge creation.

Potential

Ikujiro Nonaka's "A Dynamic Theory of Organizational Knowledge Creation" is widely considered a seminal text and its significance in the current development of academia is seldom disputed. Thus, even if in the future Nonaka's work loses its central position in academic research, it has high potential of sustaining its significance. There are many reasons to justify this stance.

First, Nonaka's knowledge conversion model, founded on the constant social interaction within and outside organizations, is believed to be a valuable starting point for the further exploration of the field of knowledge creation and organizational learning. Indeed, his article has been cited in more than 14,000 publications—an enormous accomplishment. The number of citations is not only a major factor representing the extensive recognition for the work, but also establishes the endurance of Nonaka's logic within the scholarly community. The continued interest in "A Dynamic Theory of Organizational Knowledge Creation" suggests the transitivity of the author's research

> **“**By concentrating on the concept of organizational knowledge creation, it has been possible to develop a perspective which goes beyond straightforward notions of "organizational learning. **”**
>
> Ikujiro Nonaka, "A Dynamic Theory of Organizational Knowledge Creation"

ideas.

Second, Nonaka is widely respected in the field. For instance, influential publications like *The Economist* have described Nonaka as a "management guru" in acknowledgment of his fruitful research and overall contribution to the field of knowledge creation. This not only reinforced his high standing in the scholarly community, but also charted the positive future of his research ideas, which are likely to continue to be adopted by scholars. In this manner, Nonaka may have a long-lasting influence over the course of development in the knowledge management field.

The tendency to build upon Nonaka's seminal work "A Dynamic Theory of Organizational Knowledge Creation" is strengthened by the ongoing development of the article's core ideas. Nonaka states that the SECI modes of knowledge within the organization, and between the organization and the environment, enable the knowledge creation process. The newer developments include levelling up the knowledge conversion on a more macro-institutional level. The new perspective views industry, university, and government as active parties in a collaborative process that naturally leads to more efficient national economies through knowledge development and refinement. Thus, we can expect ongoing research developments that build on, rather than deny, Nonaka's knowledge creation ideas. In that way, the relevance of Nonaka's pivotal work is expected to persist.

Future Directions

Looking ahead, Nonaka's central question—how does an organization process knowledge and is new knowledge created—continues to be relevant today. The answer to this question has contributed to a set of processes through which companies can operate with information more efficiently. A core idea that the author introduced in this discussion is the transition from knowledge as an *input to* organizations into knowledge as an *output from* organizations. This transition suggests the higher collaboration between organizations and the environments in which they operate.

Providing the theoretical reasons for collaboration, Nonaka attracted the attention of multiple parties who facilitated the realization of the prescribed knowledge creation direction; a process including the socialization, externalization, combination, and internalization of knowledge. Such parties influenced by Nonaka's core ideas include politicians, company leaders, and academics.

As a result, it is now more widely understood that the successful operation within a knowledge society needs to be an output of a collective action undertaken by and between universities, industries, and governments. This triadic relationship has been called the Triple Helix* model of collaboration.

The socialization, externalization, combination, and internalization of knowledge between these institutions is believed to lead to more efficient economies. This is because the enhanced collaboration between these interested parties can result in the better calibration of expectation from each party. Under the triple helix model, industries are the trajectory of production, universities are a spring of new commercialized knowledge, and governments the locus of contractual regulations that assure stable interaction and exchange.

Although the knowledge exchange ideas introduced by Nonaka have gone beyond the confines of academia and have permeated everyday life, it cannot be claimed that the general public is well-acquainted with them. Nevertheless, the topic of the socialization, externalization, combination, and internalization of knowledge on an institutional level remains of high political, managerial, and academic significance. This is due to triple helix's significant implications for the speeding up of the innovation and learning processes, both important for the successful operation in a contemporary knowledge-based society.

Summary

In the final analysis, Ikujiro Nonaka's "A Dynamic Theory of Organizational Knowledge Creation" deserves special attention as it frames an important area of discussion: that of knowledge creation. The research stream to which Nonaka contributes is significant for academics and business practitioners interested in promoting sustainable organizational knowledge management and economic growth.

The author introduces a dynamic model of organizational knowledge creation. This model encompasses core behavioral assumptions of how the flow of knowledge transfers between individuals, what the potential difficulties might be, and how this flow can be promoted within an organizational setting. The theoretical model thus introduced possesses sound implications for management practitioners. The model is generally intuitive, and clearly exemplifies the different types of knowledge within organizational systems, namely explicit and tacit.

Nonaka proposes that it is not only the original knowledge that is valuable, but also the subsequent one, shaped by the intra-organizational processes: socialization, externalization, combination, and internalization. This stance quickly became the standard perspective in the knowledge management field. Its importance and relevance is continuously growing due to the increasing number of citations of Nonaka's work. As mention earlier, the current number of citations of this article is more than 14,000,[1] a clear indication that no work in the field of knowledge management can be complete without utilizing Nonaka's theoretical contribution.

NOTES

1   More than 14,000 citations upon a Google Scholar search.

GLOSSARY

GLOSSARY OF TERMS

ACT: Adaptive Control of Thought, a model developed by J. Anderson that distinguishes between knowledge by diving it into *declarative knowledge* (i.e., actual knowledge) and *procedural knowledge* (i.e., methodological knowledge such as riding a bike).

Autonomy: the right of self-governance. Allowing individuals to act autonomously often stimulates the development of unexpected interpretations, solutions, etc.

Ba: Japanese word for 'place,' it signifies the importance of the shared context for knowledge creation.

Cognitive skills: skills we need to carry out any task from the simplest to the most complex. These skills are responsible for how we learn, remember, solve problems, and pay attention.

Combination: entails the enrichment of explicit knowledge and the resulting generation of more profound explicit knowledge. Combination builds upon a certain set of knowledge by integrating other relevant knowledge into it.

Competing Values Framework (CVF): a theory by Quinn Rohrbaugh that suggests the indicators of effective organizations.

Competitive advantage: refers to a condition or circumstance that puts a company in a favorable or superior business position.

Declarative knowledge: refers to factual knowledge and information that a person knows (i.e., actual knowledge).

Dynamic capabilities: defined by D. Teece as "the ability to integrate, build, and reconfigure internal and external competences to address rapidly changing environments."

Explicit knowledge: codified knowledge that is easy to transfer to another person via writing or speech, without losing information.

Externalization: entails the conversion of tacit knowledge into explicit knowledge, as this is an easier to understand form of knowledge that facilitates the transfer of personal and professional knowledge to others. J. Raelin gives the example of a professor's knowledge, which needs to be externalized in order for the students to have a full grasp on the presented material.

Fluctuation: allow individuals to question the validity of established organizational practices, structures, and routines.

Information: facts provided or learned about something or someone.

Intention: refers to an aim or a plan. It increases individuals' action orientation and motivates them to make sense of their environment.

Internalization: refers to the conversion of explicit knowledge into tacit knowledge. In internalization, action and practice are the main holders of explicit knowledge.

Job rotation: A management strategy for improving individuals' awareness of the holistic operations of organizations. The strategy is realized by assigning individuals on different positions in the company.

Knowledge society: This notion represents the continuously increasing importance of knowledge in the contemporary socio-economic environment.

Knowledge: refers to interpreted information: skills acquired through experience or education; the theoretical or practical understanding of a subject.

Organizational capabilities: the ability to effectively manage resources, such as employees, to gain an advantage over competitors.

Organizational learning: the process of creating, retaining, and transferring knowledge within an organization.

Procedural knowledge: methodological knowledge (e.g., riding a bike).

SECI: refers to socialization, externalization, combination and internalization. See their specific glossary entries.

Semiology: relates to linguistics. The study of meaning-making through the investigation of signs in the speech that indicate aspects such as symbolism, significance, attitude, etc. The objective of semiology is to improve clarity and allow classification of information systems (e.g., concepts, theories, etc.).

Socialization: refers to the transfer between an individual's tacit knowledge to another's. Individuals' knowledge is gradually transferred to the group and eventually melts in the organizational knowledge. That relocation takes place in the course of the social blend of the members via habitual interaction and through sharing the same organizational beliefs and routines. Not only does the internal socialization help in the transfer of tacit knowledge, but also through participation in joint activities or simply sharing the same.

Tacit knowledge: refers to uncodified knowledge, which is difficult to transfer, e.g., emotions, consciousness.

Triple helix: the concept of the Triple Helix of university-industry-government relationships initiated in 1993 by Etzkowitz (1993), which interprets the shift from a dominating industry-government dyad in the Industrial Society to a growing triadic relationship between university-industry-government in the Knowledge Society.

Unidirectional: allowing movement/change in all directions.

Unlearning: discarding something learned, especially a bad habit or false or outdated information from one's memory.

World War II (Second World War): a global war that lasted from 1939 to 1945.

PEOPLE MENTIONED IN THE TEXT

Alvin Toffler (1928 – 2016) was an American writer, futurist, and businessman known for his works discussing modern technologies, including the digital revolution and the communication revolution, with emphasis on their effects on cultures worldwide. Toffler was an associate editor of *Fortune* magazine.

Arie Y. Lewin (b. 1935) is professor of business administration at The Fuqua School of Business, Duke University, director of the Center for International Business Education and Research (CIBER), and editor in chief of the *Journal of International Business Studies*.

B. L. T. Hedberg is a scholar known for his contribution to the organization learning field. He has explored how organizations learn and unlearn.

C. Otto Scharmer is a professor at the Massachusetts Institute of Technology; founding chair of the Presencing Institute; and supporter of the U Theory, which is the belief that the quality of the results that we create in any kind of social system is a function of the quality of awareness, attention, or consciousness that the participants in the system operate from.

Chris Argyris (1923 – 2013) was an American business theorist, Professor Emeritus at Harvard Business School, and held the position of "Thought Leader" at consulting company Monitor Group.

Daniel Bell (1919 – 2011) was an American sociologist, writer, editor, and professor at Harvard University, best known for his contributions to the study of post-industrialism.

Daniel Tammet (b. 1979) is an English essayist, novelist, translator, and autistic savant.

David Teece (b. 1948) is a US-based organizational theorist and the Professor in Global Business and director of the Tusher Center for the Management of Intellectual Capital at the Walter A. Haas School of Business at the University of California, Berkeley.

Donald Schön (1930 - 1997) was a philosopher and professor in urban planning at the Massachusetts Institute of Technology who developed the concept of reflective practice and contributed to the theory of organizational learning.

Heinz Von Foerster (1911 - 2002) was an Austrian American scientist combining physics and philosophy, and widely acknowledged as the originator of second-order cybernetics.

Hirotaka Takeuchi (b. 1946) is a Professor in the Strategy Unit at Harvard Business School. Prior to his academic career, he worked at McCann-Erickson in Tokyo and San Francisco and at McKinsey & Company in Tokyo.

Iain Densten is a Professor of Leadership and Director of the MBA Inernational at Monash University.

Irma Becerra Fernandez is a Cuban-American higher-education leader who currently serves as the Provost and Chief Academic Officer at St. Thomas University, a non-profit, private university located in Miami, Florida.

John Robert Anderson (b. 1947) is a Canadian-born American psychologist. He is currently professor of Psychology and Computer Science at Carnegie Mellon University.

Joseph A. Raelin (b. 1948) is a Professor of Management and Organizational Development at Northeastern University Business School. His research has centered on executive and professional education and development.

Judy H. Gray is a Director of Graduate Studies at Monash University, Melbourne, Australia. Her research has been exploring the leadership development process.

K. Umemoto a scholar who have collaborated with I. Nonaka and has contributed to the organizational knowledge management field.

Kairit Tammets: a scholar from Tallinn University, Estonia, who wrote the article "Meta-Analysis of Nonaka & Takeuchi's Knowledge Management Model In The Context Of Lifelong Learning".

Karl Polanyi (1886 - 1964) was an Austro-Hungarian economic historian, economic anthropologist, economic sociologist, political economist, historical sociologist, and social philosopher. He is known for his opposition to traditional economics.

Ken Kusunoki (b. 1964) is Professor in Strategy at Hitotsubashi University. He actively contributed to the organization science research field.

Maltiadis Lytras: an academic working at the American College of Greece, in the department of Management Information Systems.

Miltiadis Lytras (b. 1973) is a Professor in the American College of Greece, Deree College. His research has contributed to the knowledge management field.

Noboru Konno is President of Knowledge Innovation Research Organization, President of Japan Innovation Network, and Professor of Tama Graduate School, Specially Appointed Professor for New Era Office Center at Kyoto Institute of Technology.

Paul S. Adler is Professor of Management and Organization at the Marshall School of Business, University of Southern California, where he holds the Harold Quinton Chair in Business Policy.

Peter Drucker (1909 – 2005) was an Austrian-born American management consultant, educator, and author, whose writings contributed to the philosophical and practical foundations of the modern business corporation. He was also a leader in the development of management education.

Philip H. Mirvis (b. 1951) is an organizational psychologist and faculty member at Boston College, in the Center for Corporate Citizenship. He has written ten books on topics on large-scale organizational change, corporate governance, and the characteristics of the workforce and workplace.

Rajiv Sabherwal is a Professor in Information Systems at Walton College.

René Jorna (b. 1953) is a researcher who contributed to the organizational knowledge management field with his research focused on knowledge management.

Ryoko Toyama served as a Research Associate of Japan Advanced Institute of Science and Technology since April 1998 and is an Associate Professor since April 2001. She has worked closely with I. Nonaka and contributed to the knowledge management research field.

WORKS CITED

WORKS CITED

"AIB Fellow - Ikujiro Nonaka," Academy of International Business (AIB), accessed April 2, 2014, http://aib.msu.edu/Fellow/192/Ikujiro-Nonaka.

Adler. "Comment on I. Nonaka: Managing innovation as an organizational knowledge creation process." In J. Allouche and G. Pogorel, (Eds), *Technology Management and Corporate Strategies: a Tricontinental Perspective.* (Amsterdam: Elsevier, 1995:110).

Anderson, J. R. *The Architecture of Cognition.* Cambridge: Harvard University Press, 1983.

Argyris, C. and Schön, D.A. *Organizational Learning.* Reading: Addison-Wesley Pub. Co., 1978.

Ashby, W. R. *An introduction to Cybernetics.* London: Champan & Hall, 1956.

Becerra-Fernandez, I. and Leidner, D. "On Knowledge, Knowledge Management, and Knowledge Systems: An Introduction: A Knowledge Management Perspective." In *Knowledge Management: An Evolutionary View,* edited by I. Becerra-Fernandez and D. Leidner. Armonk, NY: M. E. Sharpe Inc., 2008.

Becerra-Fernandez, I. and Sabherwal, R. "Individual, Group, and Organizational Learning: A Knowledge Management Perspective." In *Knowledge Management: An Evolutionary View,* edited by I. Becerra-Fernandez and D. Leidner. Armonk, NY: M. E. Sharpe Inc., 2008.

Bell, D. *The Coming of Post-industrial Society; a Venture in Social Forecasting.* New York: Basic Books, 1973.

Bereiter, C. *Education and Mind in the Knowledge Age.* Mahwah, N.J.: L. Erlbaum Associates, 2002.

Drucker, P. F. *The Age of Discontinuity; Guidelines to Our Changing Society.* New York: Harper & Row, 1969.

Easterby-Smith, M. "Organizational Learning and National Culture: Do Models of Organizational Learning Apply Ooutside the USA?." *Boletin de Estudios Economicos* 53/164 (1998): 281-296.

Easterby-Smith, M. and Lyles, M. "Introduction: Watersheds of Organizational Learning and Knowledge Management." In *The Blackwell Handbook of Organizational Learning and Knowledge Management,* edited by M. Easterby-Smith and M. Lyles, 1-15. Oxford: Blackwell Publishing, 2003.

Erden, Z., Krogh, G. and Nonaka, I. "The Quality of Group Tacit Knowledge". *Journal of Strategic Information Systems* 17 (2008): 4-18.

Essers, J. and Schreinemakers, J. "Nonaka's Subjectivist Conception of Knowledge in Corporate Knowledge Program." *Knowledge Organization* 24/1 (1997): 24-32.

Glisby, M. and Holden, N. "Contextual Constraints in Knowledge Management Theory: The Cultural Embeddedness of Nonaka's Knowledge Creating Company." *Knowledge and Process Management* 10/1 (2003): 29-36.

Gourlay, S. "Towards Conceptual Clarity for 'Tacit Knowledge': A Review of Empirical Studies." *Knowledge Management Research & Practice* 4 (2006): 60–69.

Gray, J. H. and Densten, I. L. "Towards an Integrative Model of Organizational Culture and Knowledge Management." *International Journal of Organizational Behavior* 9/2 (2005): 594-603.

Gruber, T. R. *The Acquisition of Strategic Knowledge.* Boston: Academic Press, 1989.

Hansen, M. T., Nohria, N. and Tierney, T. "What's Your Strategy for Managing Knowledge?" *Harvard Business Review* 3/4 (1995): 106-116.

Hedberg, B. L. T. "How Organizations Learn and Unlearn," in *Handbook of Organizational Design*, edited by P. C. Nystrom and W. H. Starbuck. Oxford: Oxford University Press, 1987.

Hong, J. "Glocalizing Nonaka's Knowledge Creation Model: Issues and Challenges." *Management Learning* 0 (2011): 1 –17.

Huff, A.S. (Ed.) *Mapping Strategic Thought.* Chichester: Wiley, 1990.

Jorna, R. "Managing Knowledge." *Semiotic Review of Books* 9/2 (1998): 5-8.

Kodama, M. "Knowledge Creation through Networked Strategic Communities: Case Studies on New Product Development in Japanese Companies." *Long Range Planning* 38 (2005): 27-49.

Krogh, G., Ichijo , K. and Nonaka, I. *Enabling Knowledge Creation: How to Unlock the Mystery of Tacit Knowledge and Release the Power of Innovation.* Oxford: Oxford University Press, 2000.

Lytras, M. D., Naeve, A. and Pouloudi, A. "Knowledge Management as a Reference Theory for E-learning: A Conceptual and Technological Perspective." *International Journal of Distance Education Technologies* 3/2 (2005): 1–12.

Mirvis, Philip H. "Historical foundations of organization learning." *Journal of Organizational Change Management* 9/1 (1996): 13-31.

Nonaka, I. "A Dynamic Theory of Organizational Knowledge Creation." *Organization Science* 5/1 (1994): 14-37.

Nonaka, I. and Konno, N. "The Concept of 'Ba': Building a Foundation for Knowledge Creation." *California Management Review* 40/3 (1998): 40-54.

Nonaka, I. and Takeuchi, H. *The Knowledge-creating Company: How Japanese Companies Create the Dynamics of Innovation*. New York: Oxford University Press, 1995.

Nonaka, I. and Teece, D. J. *Managing Industrial Knowledge: Creation Transfer and Utilisation*. London: SAGE, 2001.

Nonaka, I. and Toyama, R. "The Knowledge-Creating Theory Revisited: Knowledge Creation as a Synthesizing Process." *Knowledge Management Research & Practice* 1 (2003): 2-10.

Nonaka, I., Toyama, R. and Konno, N. "SECI, 'Ba' and Leadership: A Unified Model of Dynamic Knowledge Creation." *Long Range Planning* 33 (2000): 5-34.

Polanyi, M. *Personal Knowledge; Towards a Post-Critical Philosophy*. Chicago: University of Chicago Press, 1958.

Probst, G., Büchel, B. and Raub, S. "Knowledge as a strategic resource." In *Knowing in Firms*, edited by G. Von Krogh, J. Roos and D. Kleine. London: SAGE, 1998.

Raelin, J. "Work-based learning in practice." *Journal of Workplace Learning* 10 (1997): 280-283.

Sabherwal, R. and Becerra-Fernandez, I. "An Empirical Study of the Effect of Knowledge Management Processes at Individual, Group, and Organizational Levels." *Decision Sciences* 34/2 (2003): 225-311.

Sarayreh, B., Mardawi, A. and Dmour, R. "Comparative Study: The Nonaka Model of Knowledge Management." *International Journal of Engineering and Advanced Technology* 1/6 (2012): 2249 – 8958.

Scharmer, C. O. "Conversation with Ikujiro Nonaka." *Reflections: The SoL Journal* 2/2 (2000): 24-31.

Senge, P. *The Fifth Discipline*. New York, NY: Doubleday, 1990

Senge, P., Roberts, C., Ross, R., Smith, B. and Kleiner, A. *The Fifth Discipline Fieldbook*. New York, NY: Doubleday, 1994.

Skyrme, D. "Developing A Knowledge Strategy: From Management to Leadership." In *Knowledge Management: Classic and Contemporary Works*, edited by D. Morey, M. Maybury, and B. Thuraisigham, 3-61. Cambridge: MIT Press, 2000.

Tammets, K. "Meta-Analysis of Nonaka & Takeuchi's Knowledge Management Model in the Context of Lifelong Learning." *Journal of Knowledge Management Practice* 13/4 (2012): 1-15.

Teece, D. "Foreword: From the management of R and D to knowledge." In *Managing Flow: A Process Theory of the Knowledge-based Firm*, edited by I. Nonaka, R. Toyama and T. Hirata 3, New York: Palgarve MacMillan, 2008.

Teece, D. J., Pisano, G. and Shuen, A. "Dynamic Capabilities and Strategic Management." *Strategic Management Journal* 18/7 (1997): 509–533.

Toffler, A. *Powershift: Knowledge, Wealth, and Violence at the Edge of the 21st Century*. New York: Bantam Books, 1990.

Von Foerster, H. "Principles of Self-organization in a Socio-Managerial Context." In *Self-organization and Management of Social Systems*, edited by H. Ulrich and G. J.B. Probst. Berlin: Springer-Verlag, 1984.

Von Krogh, G. "Care In Knowledge Creation." *California Management Review* 40 (1998): 133-153.

Yeh, Y. C., Huang, L. Y. and Yeh, Y. L. "Knowledge Management in Blended Learning: Effects on Professional Development in Creativity Instruction." *Computers & Education* 56 (2011): 146–156.

THE MACAT LIBRARY
BY DISCIPLINE

AFRICANA STUDIES

Chinua Achebe's *An Image of Africa: Racism in Conrad's Heart of Darkness*
W. E. B. Du Bois's *The Souls of Black Folk*
Zora Neale Huston's *Characteristics of Negro Expression*
Martin Luther King Jr's *Why We Can't Wait*
Toni Morrison's *Playing in the Dark: Whiteness in the American Literary Imagination*

ANTHROPOLOGY

Arjun Appadurai's *Modernity at Large: Cultural Dimensions of Globalisation*
Philippe Ariès's *Centuries of Childhood*
Franz Boas's *Race, Language and Culture*
Kim Chan & Renée Mauborgne's *Blue Ocean Strategy*
Jared Diamond's *Guns, Germs & Steel: the Fate of Human Societies*
Jared Diamond's *Collapse: How Societies Choose to Fail or Survive*
E. E. Evans-Pritchard's *Witchcraft, Oracles and Magic Among the Azande*
James Ferguson's *The Anti-Politics Machine*
Clifford Geertz's *The Interpretation of Cultures*
David Graeber's *Debt: the First 5000 Years*
Karen Ho's *Liquidated: An Ethnography of Wall Street*
Geert Hofstede's *Culture's Consequences: Comparing Values, Behaviors, Institutes and Organizations across Nations*
Claude Lévi-Strauss's *Structural Anthropology*
Jay Macleod's *Ain't No Makin' It: Aspirations and Attainment in a Low-Income Neighborhood*
Saba Mahmood's *The Politics of Piety: The Islamic Revival and the Feminist Subject*
Marcel Mauss's *The Gift*

BUSINESS

Jean Lave & Etienne Wenger's *Situated Learning*
Theodore Levitt's *Marketing Myopia*
Burton G. Malkiel's *A Random Walk Down Wall Street*
Douglas McGregor's *The Human Side of Enterprise*
Michael Porter's *Competitive Strategy: Creating and Sustaining Superior Performance*
John Kotter's *Leading Change*
C. K. Prahalad & Gary Hamel's *The Core Competence of the Corporation*

CRIMINOLOGY

Michelle Alexander's *The New Jim Crow: Mass Incarceration in the Age of Colorblindness*
Michael R. Gottfredson & Travis Hirschi's *A General Theory of Crime*
Richard Herrnstein & Charles A. Murray's *The Bell Curve: Intelligence and Class Structure in American Life*
Elizabeth Loftus's *Eyewitness Testimony*
Jay Macleod's *Ain't No Makin' It: Aspirations and Attainment in a Low-Income Neighborhood*
Philip Zimbardo's *The Lucifer Effect*

ECONOMICS

Janet Abu-Lughod's *Before European Hegemony*
Ha-Joon Chang's *Kicking Away the Ladder*
David Brion Davis's *The Problem of Slavery in the Age of Revolution*
Milton Friedman's *The Role of Monetary Policy*
Milton Friedman's *Capitalism and Freedom*
David Graeber's *Debt: the First 5000 Years*
Friedrich Hayek's *The Road to Serfdom*
Karen Ho's *Liquidated: An Ethnography of Wall Street*

John Maynard Keynes's *The General Theory of Employment, Interest and Money*
Charles P. Kindleberger's *Manias, Panics and Crashes*
Robert Lucas's *Why Doesn't Capital Flow from Rich to Poor Countries?*
Burton G. Malkiel's *A Random Walk Down Wall Street*
Thomas Robert Malthus's *An Essay on the Principle of Population*
Karl Marx's *Capital*
Thomas Piketty's *Capital in the Twenty-First Century*
Amartya Sen's *Development as Freedom*
Adam Smith's *The Wealth of Nations*
Nassim Nicholas Taleb's *The Black Swan: The Impact of the Highly Improbable*
Amos Tversky's & Daniel Kahneman's *Judgment under Uncertainty: Heuristics and Biases*
Mahbub Ul Haq's *Reflections on Human Development*
Max Weber's *The Protestant Ethic and the Spirit of Capitalism*

FEMINISM AND GENDER STUDIES

Judith Butler's *Gender Trouble*
Simone De Beauvoir's *The Second Sex*
Michel Foucault's *History of Sexuality*
Betty Friedan's *The Feminine Mystique*
Saba Mahmood's *The Politics of Piety: The Islamic Revival and the Feminist Subject*
Joan Wallach Scott's *Gender and the Politics of History*
Mary Wollstonecraft's *A Vindication of the Rights of Woman*
Virginia Woolf's *A Room of One's Own*

GEOGRAPHY

The Brundtland Report's *Our Common Future*
Rachel Carson's *Silent Spring*
Charles Darwin's *On the Origin of Species*
James Ferguson's *The Anti-Politics Machine*
Jane Jacobs's *The Death and Life of Great American Cities*
James Lovelock's *Gaia: A New Look at Life on Earth*
Amartya Sen's *Development as Freedom*
Mathis Wackernagel & William Rees's *Our Ecological Footprint*

HISTORY

Janet Abu-Lughod's *Before European Hegemony*
Benedict Anderson's *Imagined Communities*
Bernard Bailyn's *The Ideological Origins of the American Revolution*
Hanna Batatu's *The Old Social Classes And The Revolutionary Movements Of Iraq*
Christopher Browning's *Ordinary Men: Reserve Police Batallion 101 and the Final Solution in Poland*
Edmund Burke's *Reflections on the Revolution in France*
William Cronon's *Nature's Metropolis: Chicago And The Great West*
Alfred W. Crosby's *The Columbian Exchange*
Hamid Dabashi's *Iran: A People Interrupted*
David Brion Davis's *The Problem of Slavery in the Age of Revolution*
Nathalie Zemon Davis's *The Return of Martin Guerre*
Jared Diamond's *Guns, Germs & Steel: the Fate of Human Societies*
Frank Dikotter's *Mao's Great Famine*
John W Dower's *War Without Mercy: Race And Power In The Pacific War*
W. E. B. Du Bois's *The Souls of Black Folk*
Richard J. Evans's *In Defence of History*
Lucien Febvre's *The Problem of Unbelief in the 16th Century*
Sheila Fitzpatrick's *Everyday Stalinism*

Eric Foner's *Reconstruction: America's Unfinished Revolution, 1863-1877*
Michel Foucault's *Discipline and Punish*
Michel Foucault's *History of Sexuality*
Francis Fukuyama's *The End of History and the Last Man*
John Lewis Gaddis's *We Now Know: Rethinking Cold War History*
Ernest Gellner's *Nations and Nationalism*
Eugene Genovese's *Roll, Jordan, Roll: The World the Slaves Made*
Carlo Ginzburg's *The Night Battles*
Daniel Goldhagen's *Hitler's Willing Executioners*
Jack Goldstone's *Revolution and Rebellion in the Early Modern World*
Antonio Gramsci's *The Prison Notebooks*
Alexander Hamilton, John Jay & James Madison's *The Federalist Papers*
Christopher Hill's *The World Turned Upside Down*
Carole Hillenbrand's *The Crusades: Islamic Perspectives*
Thomas Hobbes's *Leviathan*
Eric Hobsbawm's *The Age Of Revolution*
John A. Hobson's *Imperialism: A Study*
Albert Hourani's *History of the Arab Peoples*
Samuel P. Huntington's *The Clash of Civilizations and the Remaking of World Order*
C. L. R. James's *The Black Jacobins*
Tony Judt's *Postwar: A History of Europe Since 1945*
Ernst Kantorowicz's *The King's Two Bodies: A Study in Medieval Political Theology*
Paul Kennedy's *The Rise and Fall of the Great Powers*
Ian Kershaw's *The "Hitler Myth": Image and Reality in the Third Reich*
John Maynard Keynes's *The General Theory of Employment, Interest and Money*
Charles P. Kindleberger's *Manias, Panics and Crashes*
Martin Luther King Jr's *Why We Can't Wait*
Henry Kissinger's *World Order: Reflections on the Character of Nations and the Course of History*
Thomas Kuhn's *The Structure of Scientific Revolutions*
Georges Lefebvre's *The Coming of the French Revolution*
John Locke's *Two Treatises of Government*
Niccolò Machiavelli's *The Prince*
Thomas Robert Malthus's *An Essay on the Principle of Population*
Mahmood Mamdani's *Citizen and Subject: Contemporary Africa And The Legacy Of Late Colonialism*
Karl Marx's *Capital*
Stanley Milgram's *Obedience to Authority*
John Stuart Mill's *On Liberty*
Thomas Paine's *Common Sense*
Thomas Paine's *Rights of Man*
Geoffrey Parker's *Global Crisis: War, Climate Change and Catastrophe in the Seventeenth Century*
Jonathan Riley-Smith's *The First Crusade and the Idea of Crusading*
Jean-Jacques Rousseau's *The Social Contract*
Joan Wallach Scott's *Gender and the Politics of History*
Theda Skocpol's *States and Social Revolutions*
Adam Smith's *The Wealth of Nations*
Timothy Snyder's *Bloodlands: Europe Between Hitler and Stalin*
Sun Tzu's *The Art of War*
Keith Thomas's *Religion and the Decline of Magic*
Thucydides's *The History of the Peloponnesian War*
Frederick Jackson Turner's *The Significance of the Frontier in American History*
Odd Arne Westad's *The Global Cold War: Third World Interventions And The Making Of Our Times*

LITERATURE

Chinua Achebe's *An Image of Africa: Racism in Conrad's Heart of Darkness*
Roland Barthes's *Mythologies*
Homi K. Bhabha's *The Location of Culture*
Judith Butler's *Gender Trouble*
Simone De Beauvoir's *The Second Sex*
Ferdinand De Saussure's *Course in General Linguistics*
T. S. Eliot's *The Sacred Wood: Essays on Poetry and Criticism*
Zora Neale Huston's *Characteristics of Negro Expression*
Toni Morrison's *Playing in the Dark: Whiteness in the American Literary Imagination*
Edward Said's *Orientalism*
Gayatri Chakravorty Spivak's *Can the Subaltern Speak?*
Mary Wollstonecraft's *A Vindication of the Rights of Women*
Virginia Woolf's *A Room of One's Own*

PHILOSOPHY

Elizabeth Anscombe's *Modern Moral Philosophy*
Hannah Arendt's *The Human Condition*
Aristotle's *Metaphysics*
Aristotle's *Nicomachean Ethics*
Edmund Gettier's *Is Justified True Belief Knowledge?*
Georg Wilhelm Friedrich Hegel's *Phenomenology of Spirit*
David Hume's *Dialogues Concerning Natural Religion*
David Hume's *The Enquiry for Human Understanding*
Immanuel Kant's *Religion within the Boundaries of Mere Reason*
Immanuel Kant's *Critique of Pure Reason*
Søren Kierkegaard's *The Sickness Unto Death*
Søren Kierkegaard's *Fear and Trembling*
C. S. Lewis's *The Abolition of Man*
Alasdair MacIntyre's *After Virtue*
Marcus Aurelius's *Meditations*
Friedrich Nietzsche's *On the Genealogy of Morality*
Friedrich Nietzsche's *Beyond Good and Evil*
Plato's *Republic*
Plato's *Symposium*
Jean-Jacques Rousseau's *The Social Contract*
Gilbert Ryle's *The Concept of Mind*
Baruch Spinoza's *Ethics*
Sun Tzu's *The Art of War*
Ludwig Wittgenstein's *Philosophical Investigations*

POLITICS

Benedict Anderson's *Imagined Communities*
Aristotle's *Politics*
Bernard Bailyn's *The Ideological Origins of the American Revolution*
Edmund Burke's *Reflections on the Revolution in France*
John C. Calhoun's *A Disquisition on Government*
Ha-Joon Chang's *Kicking Away the Ladder*
Hamid Dabashi's *Iran: A People Interrupted*
Hamid Dabashi's *Theology of Discontent: The Ideological Foundation of the Islamic Revolution in Iran*
Robert Dahl's *Democracy and its Critics*
Robert Dahl's *Who Governs?*
David Brion Davis's *The Problem of Slavery in the Age of Revolution*

Alexis De Tocqueville's *Democracy in America*
James Ferguson's *The Anti-Politics Machine*
Frank Dikotter's *Mao's Great Famine*
Sheila Fitzpatrick's *Everyday Stalinism*
Eric Foner's *Reconstruction: America's Unfinished Revolution, 1863-1877*
Milton Friedman's *Capitalism and Freedom*
Francis Fukuyama's *The End of History and the Last Man*
John Lewis Gaddis's *We Now Know: Rethinking Cold War History*
Ernest Gellner's *Nations and Nationalism*
David Graeber's *Debt: the First 5000 Years*
Antonio Gramsci's *The Prison Notebooks*
Alexander Hamilton, John Jay & James Madison's *The Federalist Papers*
Friedrich Hayek's *The Road to Serfdom*
Christopher Hill's *The World Turned Upside Down*
Thomas Hobbes's *Leviathan*
John A. Hobson's *Imperialism: A Study*
Samuel P. Huntington's *The Clash of Civilizations and the Remaking of World Order*
Tony Judt's *Postwar: A History of Europe Since 1945*
David C. Kang's *China Rising: Peace, Power and Order in East Asia*
Paul Kennedy's *The Rise and Fall of Great Powers*
Robert Keohane's *After Hegemony*
Martin Luther King Jr.'s *Why We Can't Wait*
Henry Kissinger's *World Order: Reflections on the Character of Nations and the Course of History*
John Locke's *Two Treatises of Government*
Niccolò Machiavelli's *The Prince*
Thomas Robert Malthus's *An Essay on the Principle of Population*
Mahmood Mamdani's *Citizen and Subject: Contemporary Africa And The Legacy Of Late Colonialism*
Karl Marx's *Capital*
John Stuart Mill's *On Liberty*
John Stuart Mill's *Utilitarianism*
Hans Morgenthau's *Politics Among Nations*
Thomas Paine's *Common Sense*
Thomas Paine's *Rights of Man*
Thomas Piketty's *Capital in the Twenty-First Century*
Robert D. Putman's *Bowling Alone*
John Rawls's *Theory of Justice*
Jean-Jacques Rousseau's *The Social Contract*
Theda Skocpol's *States and Social Revolutions*
Adam Smith's *The Wealth of Nations*
Sun Tzu's *The Art of War*
Henry David Thoreau's *Civil Disobedience*
Thucydides's *The History of the Peloponnesian War*
Kenneth Waltz's *Theory of International Politics*
Max Weber's *Politics as a Vocation*
Odd Arne Westad's *The Global Cold War: Third World Interventions And The Making Of Our Times*

POSTCOLONIAL STUDIES

Roland Barthes's *Mythologies*
Frantz Fanon's *Black Skin, White Masks*
Homi K. Bhabha's *The Location of Culture*
Gustavo Gutiérrez's *A Theology of Liberation*
Edward Said's *Orientalism*
Gayatri Chakravorty Spivak's *Can the Subaltern Speak?*

PSYCHOLOGY

Gordon Allport's *The Nature of Prejudice*
Alan Baddeley & Graham Hitch's *Aggression: A Social Learning Analysis*
Albert Bandura's *Aggression: A Social Learning Analysis*
Leon Festinger's *A Theory of Cognitive Dissonance*
Sigmund Freud's *The Interpretation of Dreams*
Betty Friedan's *The Feminine Mystique*
Michael R. Gottfredson & Travis Hirschi's *A General Theory of Crime*
Eric Hoffer's *The True Believer: Thoughts on the Nature of Mass Movements*
William James's *Principles of Psychology*
Elizabeth Loftus's *Eyewitness Testimony*
A. H. Maslow's *A Theory of Human Motivation*
Stanley Milgram's *Obedience to Authority*
Steven Pinker's *The Better Angels of Our Nature*
Oliver Sacks's *The Man Who Mistook His Wife For a Hat*
Richard Thaler & Cass Sunstein's *Nudge: Improving Decisions About Health, Wealth and Happiness*
Amos Tversky's *Judgment under Uncertainty: Heuristics and Biases*
Philip Zimbardo's *The Lucifer Effect*

SCIENCE

Rachel Carson's *Silent Spring*
William Cronon's *Nature's Metropolis: Chicago And The Great West*
Alfred W. Crosby's *The Columbian Exchange*
Charles Darwin's *On the Origin of Species*
Richard Dawkin's *The Selfish Gene*
Thomas Kuhn's *The Structure of Scientific Revolutions*
Geoffrey Parker's *Global Crisis: War, Climate Change and Catastrophe in the Seventeenth Century*
Mathis Wackernagel & William Rees's *Our Ecological Footprint*

SOCIOLOGY

Michelle Alexander's *The New Jim Crow: Mass Incarceration in the Age of Colorblindness*
Gordon Allport's *The Nature of Prejudice*
Albert Bandura's *Aggression: A Social Learning Analysis*
Hanna Batatu's *The Old Social Classes And The Revolutionary Movements Of Iraq*
Ha-Joon Chang's *Kicking Away the Ladder*
W. E. B. Du Bois's *The Souls of Black Folk*
Émile Durkheim's *On Suicide*
Frantz Fanon's *Black Skin, White Masks*
Frantz Fanon's *The Wretched of the Earth*
Eric Foner's *Reconstruction: America's Unfinished Revolution, 1863-1877*
Eugene Genovese's *Roll, Jordan, Roll: The World the Slaves Made*
Jack Goldstone's *Revolution and Rebellion in the Early Modern World*
Antonio Gramsci's *The Prison Notebooks*
Richard Herrnstein & Charles A Murray's *The Bell Curve: Intelligence and Class Structure in American Life*
Eric Hoffer's *The True Believer: Thoughts on the Nature of Mass Movements*
Jane Jacobs's *The Death and Life of Great American Cities*
Robert Lucas's *Why Doesn't Capital Flow from Rich to Poor Countries?*
Jay Macleod's *Ain't No Makin' It: Aspirations and Attainment in a Low Income Neighborhood*
Elaine May's *Homeward Bound: American Families in the Cold War Era*
Douglas McGregor's *The Human Side of Enterprise*
C. Wright Mills's *The Sociological Imagination*

Thomas Piketty's *Capital in the Twenty-First Century*
Robert D. Putman's *Bowling Alone*
David Riesman's *The Lonely Crowd: A Study of the Changing American Character*
Edward Said's *Orientalism*
Joan Wallach Scott's *Gender and the Politics of History*
Theda Skocpol's *States and Social Revolutions*
Max Weber's *The Protestant Ethic and the Spirit of Capitalism*

THEOLOGY

Augustine's *Confessions*
Benedict's *Rule of St Benedict*
Gustavo Gutiérrez's *A Theology of Liberation*
Carole Hillenbrand's *The Crusades: Islamic Perspectives*
David Hume's *Dialogues Concerning Natural Religion*
Immanuel Kant's *Religion within the Boundaries of Mere Reason*
Ernst Kantorowicz's *The King's Two Bodies: A Study in Medieval Political Theology*
Søren Kierkegaard's *The Sickness Unto Death*
C. S. Lewis's *The Abolition of Man*
Saba Mahmood's *The Politics of Piety: The Islamic Revival and the Feminist Subject*
Baruch Spinoza's *Ethics*
Keith Thomas's *Religion and the Decline of Magic*

COMING SOON

Chris Argyris's *The Individual and the Organisation*
Seyla Benhabib's *The Rights of Others*
Walter Benjamin's *The Work Of Art in the Age of Mechanical Reproduction*
John Berger's *Ways of Seeing*
Pierre Bourdieu's *Outline of a Theory of Practice*
Mary Douglas's *Purity and Danger*
Roland Dworkin's *Taking Rights Seriously*
James G. March's *Exploration and Exploitation in Organisational Learning*
Ikujiro Nonaka's *A Dynamic Theory of Organizational Knowledge Creation*
Griselda Pollock's *Vision and Difference*
Amartya Sen's *Inequality Re-Examined*
Susan Sontag's *On Photography*
Yasser Tabbaa's *The Transformation of Islamic Art*
Ludwig von Mises's *Theory of Money and Credit*